A FLOCK OF
WORDS

A FLOCK OF WORDS

An Anthology of Poetry for
Children and Others

COLLECTED, INTRODUCED, AND
ANNOTATED BY

David Mackay

PREFACE BY

Benjamin DeMott

DRAWINGS BY

Margery Gill

HARCOURT, BRACE & WORLD, INC.
NEW YORK

R01 0898 0571

Copyright © 1969 by The Bodley Head

Library of Congress Catalog Card Number: 77-91070

Printed in the United States of America

First American edition, 1970

B C D E F G H

Every effort has been made to trace the ownership of all copyrighted material in this book and to secure the necessary permissions to reprint these selections. In the event of any question arising as to the use of any material, the publisher and the editor, while expressing regret for any inadvertent error, will be pleased to make the necessary correction in future printings. Thanks are due to the following for permission to reprint the copyrighted material listed below:

GEORGE ALLEN & UNWIN LTD. for "Getting up Early on a Spring Morning" by Po Chü-i, "Hot Cake" by Shu Hsi, "In the Mountains on a Summer Day" by Li Po, and "The Little Cart" by Ch'ên Tzŭ-lung from *Chinese Poems,* translated by Arthur Waley.

ANGUS & ROBERTSON LTD. for an extract from "Lady Feeding the Cats" by Douglas Stewart; for "The Silkworms" from *Rutherford* by Douglas Stewart; for "The Cicadas" from *The Gateway* by Judith Wright; and for "Legend" by Judith Wright.

ATHENEUM PUBLISHERS for "Fourteen Ways of Touching the Peter" from *The Night of Stones* by George MacBeth, Copyright © 1968 by George MacBeth.

BANTAM BOOKS, INC., for "Envy" by Yevtushenko, translated by George Reavey, from *Modern European Poetry,* edited by Willis Barnstone et al., Copyright © 1966, Bantam Books, Inc.

BARNES & NOBLE, INC., for "Christmas Star" and "The Zoo" from *Fifty Poems* by Boris Pasternak, translated by Lydia Pasternak.

BOWES & BOWES LTD. for "The Odyssey of a Snail" by Federico García Lorca from *Lorca: An Appreciation of His Poetry,* translated by Roy Campbell.

JONATHAN CAPE LTD. and GLYN JONES for "Perfect" by Glyn Jones. These lines (with the exception of the first) appear in the short story by Glyn Jones, "Porth-y-Rhyd," from his collection of short stories, *The Blue Bed,* published by Jonathan Cape Ltd. They have been rearranged by Hugh MacDiarmid to make the poem which he has called "Perfect."

JEROME CH'ÊN and MICHAEL BULLOCK for their translations of "The Ruined City" by Pao Chao and an extract from "Fifteen Poems of My Heart" by Juan Chi from *Poems of Solitude,* edited and translated by Jerome Ch'ên and Michael Bullock (UNESCO Collection of Representative Works, Chinese Series), Abelard-Schuman, 1960, © Jerome Ch'ên and Michael Bullock.

F. W. CHESHIRE PUBLISHING PTY. LTD. for "On My Short-Sightedness" by Prem Chaya from *Span, An Adventure in Asian and Australian Writing.*

CHILMARK PRESS INC. for an extract from "In Parenthesis" by David Jones.

CITY LIGHTS BOOKS for "To Paint the Portrait of a Bird" from *Paroles* by Jacques Prévert, translated by Lawrence Ferlinghetti, Copyright © 1947 by Les Editions du Point du Jour, Paris, first published in City Lights edition: July 1958, by arrangement with Librarie Gallimard.

THE CLARENDON PRESS, OXFORD, for "A Charm against the Stitch" from *Anglo-Saxon Poetry* by Gavin Bone.

PETER COLLENETTE for his poem "Precision."

COLLINS-KNOWLTON-WING, INC., for "Flying Crooked," "Lollocks," and "Warning to Children" from *Collected Poems 1955* by Robert Graves, Copyright © 1955 by Robert Graves.

CONSTABLE AND COMPANY LIMITED for "The Herdboy" by Lu Yu, "Pruning Trees" by Po Chü-i, and "The Eastern Gate" from *170 Chinese Poems,* translated by Arthur Waley.

CORINTH BOOKS INC. for the extract, "John Muir on Mt. Ritter," from "Burning" by Gary Snyder from *Myths and Texts,* Copyright © 1960 Gary Snyder, published by Corinth Books.

CURTIS BROWN LTD. for "A Correct Compassion" from *A Correct Compassion and Other Poems* by James Kirkup; and for "Japanese Children" and "Waiting" from *The Prodigal Son, Poems 1956-1959* by James Kirkup.

DOUBLEDAY & COMPANY, INC., for an extract from "Genesis" (*Anchor Bible*), translated and edited by E. A. Speiser, Copyright © 1964 by Doubleday & Company, Inc.; for "A trout leaps high" by Uejima Onitsura from *An Introduction to Haiku* by Harold G. Henderson, Copyright © 1958 by Harold G. Henderson; for an extract from "The Odyssey," translated by Robert Fitzgerald, Copyright © 1961 by Robert Fitzgerald; for "The Bat," Copyright 1938 by Theodore Roethke, and for "My Papa's Waltz," Copyright 1942 by Hearst Magazines, Inc., both from *The Collected Poems of Theodore Roethke.*

ENCOUNTER LIMITED for "Season" and "Telephone Conversation" by Wole Soyinka.

EYRE & SPOTTISWOODE (PUBLISHERS) LTD. for an extract from "Autumn" from *Walking Wounded* by Vernon Scannell.

FABER AND FABER LIMITED for an extract from "The Nightfishing" from *The Nightfishing* by W. S. Graham; for "My Sister Jane"

from *Happily Ever After* by Ian Serraillier; and for "The Redwoods" from *Selected Poems* by Louis Simpson.

PENGUIN BOOKS LTD. for "Disturbed, the cat," "Judging from the pictures," "Now the man has a child," "Sheltering from the rain," "The chicken wants," and "With his apology" by Karai Senryū, for "Snow melting!" by Katō Gyōdai, for "Late Summer" by Kinoshita Yūji, for "Rain on Castle Island" by Kitahara Hakushū, for "Red sky in the morning" and "Stop! don't swat the fly" by Kobayashi Issa, for "A heavy cart rumbles" by Kuroyanagi Shōha, for "On a bare branch" by Matsuo Bashō, for "I've seen everything" by Naitō Josō, for "The wind blows grey" by Naitō Meisetsu, for "Then settle, frost!" by Ōtomo Ōemaru, for an extract from "Poems of Solitary Delights" by Tachibana Akemi, for "Against the broad sky," "In the old man's eyes," "On far hills," and "The snake fled" by Takahama Kyoshi, for "Winter withering" by Tan Taigi, for "Silent, but . . ." by Tsuboi Shigeji, for "The noisy cricket" by Watanabe Suiha, for "Scampering over saucers" by Yosa Buson, for "Folk Song from Fukushima" and "Looking at the moon on putting out from the shore at Nagato," all from ·*The Penguin Book of Japanese Verse* (1964), translated by Geoffrey Bownas and Anthony Thwaite; for "Chopsticks" by Yüan Mei from *The Penguin Book of Chinese Verse*, translated by Robert Kotewall and Norman L. Smith; for an extract from *The Canterbury Tales* by Geoffrey Chaucer, translated by Nevill Coghill; for lines 199-225 from "Beowulf" from *The Earliest English Poems*, translated by Michael Alexander; for "A Boy's Head" and "A History Lesson" by Miroslav Holub from *Selected Poems of Miroslav Holub*, translated by Ian Milner and George Theiner; for "Alleyway" by Salvatore Quasimodo from *Selected Verse of Quasimodo*, translated by Jack Bevan; for "The Panther" by R. M. Rilke from *Selected Poems*, translated by J. B. Leishman; for "Flowers," an extract from "Phrases," and "The Bridges" from "Les Illuminations" from *Selected Verse* by Jean-Nicolas-Arthur Rimbaud, translated by Oliver Bernard; for "Travelling through the Dark" by William Stafford from *The Penguin Book of Contemporary American Poetry*, edited by Curtis Zahn; for "The Companion" and "Schoolmaster" by Yevgeny Yevtushenko from *Selected Verse of Yevtushenko*, translated by Robin Milner-Gulland and Peter Levi.

A. D. PETERS & CO. for lines 311-392 from Book I, for lines 328-345 from Book II, and for lines 1-41 and 51-57 from Book IV of *The Georgics of Virgil*, translated by C. Day Lewis.

PRÉSENCE AFRICAINE, Paris, for "Omen" by Birago Diop, first published in the anthology of Birago Diop entitled *Leurres et lueurs*.

RANDOM HOUSE, INC., for "Elegy for J.F.K.," "Postscript," and two extracts from "Symmetries and Asymmetries" from *About the House* by W. H. Auden, © copyright 1965 by W. H. Auden; for "O What is that Sound" and "On This Island" by W. H. Auden, Copyright 1937 and renewed 1965 by W. H. Auden, reprinted from *Collected Shorter*

FOR MARY AND JANET

CONTENTS

Preface

by Professor Benjamin DeMott
Chairman of the English Department at
Amherst College, Massachusetts

Hard not to be florid about this book . . . Tasted in snippets or read straight through, it offers extraordinary experiences. Because David Mackay has a superbly subtle feeling for the idea of a 'subject' in a poem, the juxtapositions of pieces in these pages seem actually to create whole new themes for meditation. Read along and the dawnings multiply—feelings, places, situations hitherto unrelated are now all hooks-and-eyes into each other. And because Mr Mackay finds his poets over the lot, every continent, a dozen languages, you touch the truth hidden in weary phrases about the 'universality of poetry'. Man is the poet here, not English man or Japanese man or American man, but general man 'belonging' to a life longer and larger than his own—the life of natural things.

And (one more pleasure worth a word): the poems in *A Flock of Words* are dense with 'aboutness'. Grouped as they are, they're seen to possess roots; their laughter or sadness or anger has visible causes. The humanness of poem-writing as an activity, the noble inevitability of it—that is what this collection teaches.

But floridity was to be avoided. One summer day—*pace* the anti-sentimentalists: life is short—I sat in the sun by a New Hampshire brook with a friend and passed pages of this manuscript back and forth, reading bits aloud, chuckling or looking grave, sometimes bemused. A while back, this was, yet I remember no happier afternoon. Delicious memory, lovely book!

Introduction

Some years ago now, this book began as a collection of cuttings from papers and pages copied out by hand from books I could not then afford to buy. The collection was a precious possession—the more so because the poems, and often the poets, were new to me. In choosing them, I was finally asserting my own taste in poetry over that which I had acquired uneasily in the course of a public education. The poems gathered in this way came from many different ages and from many different places: there were poems originally written in English and poems translated into modern English: poems from ancient literary traditions, and poems newly published by living poets and waiting for readers. Some of these were taken into the classroom, and the most successful stayed there and became the nucleus of this book. Most of them had not been written for young readers: they were written, as far as I knew, for anyone who cared to read them.

A Flock of Words grew also as a challenge to the whimsical, ineffectual school books that seemed to give so many children printed proof of the fact that poetry was not only daft but boring. Poetry as a school subject became exciting for *us* (for me as the teacher and the children I was teaching) only when professional poets were listened to; and they alone gave us ideas about the nature of poetry. With little encouragement some children were activated by similar interests and similar processes to those that had sent a poet off to write. All the talk about poets, poems and us which then developed, was to become a strong influence on how the children were to write. Nor were they too much in awe of the professionals to emulate some of them. This did not always succeed in producing good writing, but it was always instructive and sometimes exciting. Gradually it led to a closer look at the way a poet converts thoughts, feelings and events into the language of literature. For fleeting moments in the midst of hectic schooldays children knew the elation of making a piece of writing work. We learned to be patient with our expectations of what poetry was like and what it should do. We would return to a poem more than once, each time with the likelihood of greater enjoyment and understanding, leaving the patterns of its sounds, its images, its thoughts and feelings to work inside us in their own way. Of course there were many more things to do in a day than listen to poetry or write it or read it. But nothing gave us more to think about or set us talking so readily or taught us more about ourselves and our fellow men.

Living with a growing collection of poems meant that they were constantly being rearranged. Sometimes they reflected our seasonal interests; sometimes collections were made to enable us to reveal aspects of 'the human situation', the elements, everyday events, war, animals and so on. These poems rubbed shoulders together and often changed places according to our whims or to the way we discovered that they related to one another—by similarity or contrast—and heightened our interest in a subject by their proximity. The form in which the poems appear here is an extension of this.

Although in one sense *A Flock of Words* is not for anyone in particular, its most important readers have always been envisaged as young people who will read it and have it read to them over and over again during the whole period of their growing up. It is for them that notes and sources have been added so that they may follow up a poet's work and explore other anthologies (a search in which all librarians will be glad to join). Using the book in this way as a base from which to plan explorations, they will discover some of its omissions and may gradually come to share fully what, for the time being, does not interest them.

A Flock of Words was made out of the confrontation of people and poetry. A poem is there because it concerned the young audience who heard it and because by contact with it their sympathies were enlarged. Of course this happens in many different ways—from the sensitive reactions to disaster, sadness, beauty, ugliness and magic, to the smiles and laughter which comical things compel in us.

For children everything is new. No names are famous for them. Indeed, to begin with, all poets are anonymous (and may remain so throughout the lives of some). Only with the growing affection for, and familiarity with, a poem will they turn to ask who wrote it. Before this they will ask for 'the one about the horse, the storm or the death of King Arthur'. It is the subject that matters: a poem must stand or fall by its own virtue. It will be read or listened to willingly only because it is compelling and effective. The poems in this book were chosen because they proved to have these qualities and because they were found to satisfy some of the changing and changeable moods and tastes of young people growing up.

Children and adults have appetites that are both fine and coarse, and their growing sensitivity is neither confused nor blunted by exposure to the good, the bad and the indifferent. Indeed there is no other way in which positive attitudes to literature can adequately develop than by constantly setting up for comparison literary and non-literary works and making judgments about their virtues and their appropriate places in our lives. To be confronted with exclusive diets of tinsel *or* grandeur is intolerable and unhealthy, but the tinsel is always more easily come by and is easy to read. Children have very little access to adult literature and no hope of selecting from it what is of interest to them, so that it is always necessary to have someone who is prepared to sift and select from a mass of published works the small share of adult literature they properly should have. It is also necessary for them to have a sympathetic adult around, with whom they can discuss their reactions to such works. This implies that those of us who undertake to do this will not under-rate their interests and understanding, nor presume to know with too much certainty what is good for them.

For this reason *A Flock of Words* is wide-ranging in subject, time and place. It attempts no exclusiveness. It does not seek to create a rarefied poetic atmosphere. In it the meaning of poetry has been widely interpreted, and the poet is seen, not as a national monument set in a cathedral niche, but as a writer whose work, whatever his nationality, whatever the year in which he lived, has the power to convey to us *now* some of the experiences that shaped him and which shape us too.

No anthology is more than a fragment that reflects the personal predilections and private purposes of its compiler. For readers who find the following pages too eclectic, I offer no apology; in this respect a difference of taste and interest is likely to be as much an asset as any of the other ways in which the variety of life is expressed. In the end it is not the anthology that is important but the poets whose works it samples and the readers who come under its influence.

The poems on sheets of paper continued to grow in number as

colleagues and friends shared new poems with me. But the day arrives when the feeling grows that a whole book is there, and that all that remains to be done to make it complete is finally to order its contents in the best possible way. Much of the present arrangement was derived from the sequences of poems that had proved exciting and revealing in classroom use—in which a good deal of intuition had been at work: the results of which the reader will discover in the following pages.

Where modernisation of spelling and punctuation does not otherwise alter a poem, this has been done: one convention has been exchanged for another to ease communication. Archaic and dialect words have been glossed in the notes and given their most appropriate modern equivalents.

My thanks are due to many people who have helped to make this book; to the young men and women, who, as children, were the first to listen to it and who were its first readers; to the poets who have given permission for their work to be published in this way; to the publishers for having made this a beautiful book; and lastly to all the friends with whom I have read and discussed poetry and from whom I learned of new poems, some of which are included here. To none of these do I owe more than to my colleague Brian Thompson who, from his voracious reading and his enthusiasm for poetry, gave me access to what I believe to have been some rare finds.

David Mackay
London, 1968

A FLOCK OF
WORDS

from Genesis

When God set about to create heaven and earth—the world being then a formless waste, with darkness over the seas and only an awesome wind sweeping over the water—God said, 'Let there be light.' And there was light. God was pleased with the light that he saw, and he separated the light from the darkness. God called the light Day, and he called the darkness Night. Thus evening came, and morning—first day.

God said, 'Let there be an expanse in the middle of the water to form a division between the waters.' And it was so. God made the expanse, and it divided the water below it from the water above it. God called the expanse Sky. Thus evening came, and morning—second day.

God said, 'Let the water beneath the sky be gathered into a single area, that the dry land may be visible.' And it was so.

God called the dry land Earth, and he called the gathered waters Seas. God was pleased with what he saw, and he said, 'Let the earth burst forth with growth: plants that bear seed, and every kind of fruit tree on earth that bears fruit with its seed in it.' And it was so. The earth produced growth: various kinds of seed-bearing plants, and trees of every kind bearing fruit with seed in it. And God was pleased with what he saw. Thus evening came, and morning—third day.

God said, 'Let there be lights in the expanse of the sky, to distinguish between day and night; let them mark the fixed times, the days and the years, and serve as lights in the expanse of the sky to shine upon the earth.' And it was so. God made the great lights, the greater one to dominate the day and the lesser one to dominate the night—and the stars. God set them in the expanse of the sky to shine upon the earth, to dominate the day and the night, and to distinguish between light and darkness. And God was pleased with what he saw. Thus evening came, and morning—fourth day.

God said, 'Let the waters teem with swarms of living creatures, and let birds fly above the earth across the expanse of the sky.'

I

And it was so. God created the great sea monsters, every kind of crawling creature with which the waters teem, and all kinds of winged birds. And God was pleased with what he saw. God blessed them, saying, 'Be fertile and increase; fill the waters in the seas, and let the birds multiply on earth.' Thus evening came, and morning —fifth day.

God said, 'Let the earth bring forth various kinds of living creatures: cattle, creeping things, and wild animals of every kind.' And it was so. God made various kinds of wild animals, cattle of every kind, and all the creeping things of the earth, whatever their kind. And God was pleased with what he saw.

Then God said, 'I will make man in my image, after my likeness; let him subject the fish of the sea and the birds of the sky, the cattle and all the wild animals, and all the creatures that creep on earth.'

And God created man in his image;
In the divine image created he him,
Male and female created he them.

God blessed them, saying to them, 'Be fertile and increase, fill the earth and subdue it; subject the fishes of the sea, the birds of the sky, and all the living things that move on earth.' God further said, 'See, I give you every seed-bearing plant on earth and every tree that bears fruit; they shall be yours for food. And to all the animals on land, all the birds of the sky, and all the living creatures that crawl on earth I give all the green plants as their food.' And it was so. God looked at everything that he had made and found it very pleasing. Thus evening came, and morning—sixth day.

Now the heaven and the earth were completed, and all their company. On the seventh day God brought to a close the work that he had been doing, and he ceased on the seventh day from all the work that he had undertaken. God blessed the seventh day and declared it holy, for on it he ceased from all the work which he had undertaken.

Such is the story of heaven and earth as they were created.

Palestine, 5th century B.C.
Trans. Ephraim Avigdor Speiser

A New Year Carol

Anon.

Here we bring new water
    from the well so clear
For to worship God with,
    this happy New Year.

Sing levy dew, sing levy dew
    the water and the wine;
The seven bright gold wires
    and the bugles that do shine.

Sing reign of Fair Maid,
    with gold upon her toe,—
Open you the West Door,
    and turn the Old Year go.

Sing reign of Fair Maid
    with gold upon her chin,—
Open you the East Door,
    and let the New Year in.

Sing levy dew, sing levy dew,
    the water and the wine,
The seven bright gold wires
    and the bugles they do shine.

England, trad.

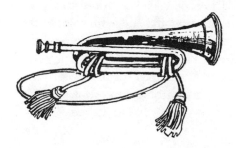

from Odes of the Months

Aneirin

Month of January—smoky is the vale;
Weary the wine-bearer; strolling the minstrel;
Lean the cow; seldom the hum of the bee;
Empty the milking fold; void of meat the kiln;
Slender the horse; very silent the bird;
Long to the early dawn; short the afternoon;
Justly spoke Cynfelyn,
'Prudence is the best guide for man.'

Wales, 6th century
Trans. W. Probert

Winter in the Fens

John Clare

So moping flat and low our valleys lie,
So dull and muggy is our winter sky,
Drizzling from day to day with threats of rain,
And when that falls still threatening on again;
From one wet week so great an ocean flows
That every village to an island grows,
And every road for even weeks to come
Is stopped, and none but horsemen go from home;
And one wet night leaves travel's best in doubt,
And horseback travellers ask if floods are out
Of every passer-by, and with their horse
The meadow's ocean try in vain to cross;
The horse's footings with a sucking sound
Fill up with water on the firmest ground,
And ruts that dribble into brooks elsewhere
Can find no fall or flat to dribble here;

4

But filled with wet they brim and overflow
Till hollows in the road to rivers grow;
Then wind with sudden rage, abrupt and blea,
Twirls every lingering leaf from off each tree.
Such is our lowland scene that winter gives,
And strangers wonder where our comfort lives;
Yet in a little close, however keen
The winter comes, I find a patch of green,
Where robins, by the miser winter made
Domestic, flirt and perch upon the spade;
And in a little garden-close at home
I watch for spring—and there's the crocus come!

England, 19th century

Shine Out Fair Sun

Anon.

Shine out fair sun, with all your heat,
Show all your thousand-coloured light!
Black Winter freezes to his sea;
The grey wolf howls he does so bite;
Crookt Age on three knees creeps the street;
The boneless fish close quaking lies
And eats for cold his aching feet;
The stars in icicles arise:
Shine out, and make this winter night
Our beauty's Spring, our Prince of light.

England, 16th century

Spring, the Sweet Spring

Thomas Nashe

Spring, the sweet spring, is the year's pleasant king;
Then blooms each thing, then maids dance in a ring,
Cold doth not sting, the pretty birds do sing,
Cuckoo, jug, jug, pu we, to witta woo.

The palm and may make country houses gay,
Lambs frisk and play, the shepherds pipe all day,
And we hear aye birds tune this merry lay,
Cuckoo, jug jug, pu we, to witta woo.

The fields breathe sweet, the daisies kiss our feet,
Young lovers meet, old wives a-sunning sit,
In every street these tunes our ears do greet,
Cuckoo, jug jug, pu we, to witta woo.

England, 16th century

Spring

Henry Howard, Earl of Surrey

The soote season, that bud and bloom forth brings,
With green hath clad the hill—and eke the vale:
The nightingale with feathers new she sings;
The turtle to her mate hath told her tale;
Summer is come, for every spray now springs.
The hart hath hung his old head on the pale;
The buck in brake his winter coat he flings;
The fishes float with new repaired scale;
The adder all her slough away she slings;
The swift swallow pursueth the flies small;
The busy bee her honey now she mings;
Winter is worn that was the flowers' bale.
　　And thus I see among these pleasant things
　　Each care decays, and yet my sorrow springs.

England, 16th century

6

By chance I walk . . .

Yüan Mei

By chance I walk into the western courtyard.
There in the shelter of the porch
A solitary orchid has flowered.
How quickly the news gets around
For already the bees are arriving.

China, 18th century
Arr. D.M.

e. e. cummings

Spring is like a perhaps hand
(which comes carefully
out of Nowhere) arranging
a window, into which people look (while
people stare
arranging and changing placing
carefully there a strange
thing and a known thing here) and

changing everything carefully

spring is like a perhaps
Hand in a window
(carefully to
and fro moving New and
Old things, while
people stare carefully
moving a perhaps
fraction of flower here placing
an inch of air there) and

without breaking anything.

U.S.A., 20th century

Tan Taigi
Winter withering:
Sparrows strut
In the guttering.

Japan, 18th century
Trans. Bownas & Thwaite

Blossom Themes

Carl Sandburg

1

Late in the winter came one day
When there was a whiff on the wind,
a suspicion, a cry not to be heard
   of perhaps blossoms, perhaps green
   grass and clean hills lifting rolling shoulders.
Does the nose get the cry of spring
   first of all? is the nose thankful
   and thrilled first of all?

2

If the blossoms come down
so they must fall on snow
because spring comes this year
before winter is gone,
then both snow and blossoms look sad;
peaches, cherries, the red summer apples,
all say it is a hard year.
The wind has its own way of picking off
the smell of peach blossoms and then
carrying that smell miles and miles.
   Women washing dishes in lonely farmhouses
   stand at the door and say, 'Something is
   happening.'

8

A little foam of the summer sea
of blossoms,
a foam finger of white leaves,
shut these away—
high into the summer wind runners.
Let the wind be white too.

U.S.A., 20th century

Getting up Early on a Spring Morning
Po Chü-i

The early light of the rising sun shines on the beams of
    my house;
The first banging of opened doors echoes like the roll of
    a drum.
The dog lies curled on the stone step, for the earth is wet
    with dew;
The birds come near to the window and chatter, telling
    that the day is fine.
With the lingering fumes of yesterday's wine my head
    is still heavy;
With new doffing of winter clothes my body has grown
    light.
I woke up with heart empty and mind utterly extinct;
Lately, for many nights on end, I have not dreamt of
    home.

China, 9th century
Trans. Arthur Waley

Katō Gyōdai

Snow melting!
Deep in the hill-mist
A crow cawing.

Japan, 18th century
Trans. Bownas & Thwaite

9

Thaw

Edward Thomas

Over the land freckled with snow half-thawed
The speculating rooks at their nests cawed
And saw from elm-tops, delicate as flowers of grass,
What we below could not see, Winter pass.

England, 20th century

To a Primrose

John Clare

Welcome, pale Primrose! starting up between
Dead matted leaves of ash and oak, that strew
The sunny lawn, the wood, the coppice through
'Mid creeping moss and ivy's darker green;
How much thy presence beautifies the ground!
How sweet thy modest, unaffected pride
Glows on the sunny bank, and wood's warm side!
And where thy fairy flowers in groups are found,
The schoolboy roams enchantedly along,
Plucking the fairest with a rude delight:
While the meek shepherd stops his simple song,
To gaze a moment on the pleasing sight;
O'erjoyed to see the flowers that truly bring
The welcome news of sweet returning Spring.

England, 19th century

The Cuckoo

Kodo

If the cuckoo were
lovely blossoms I would pluck
one sweet note from her!

Japan, 18th century
Trans. Kenneth Yasuda

Repeat that, repeat

Gerard Manley Hopkins

Repeat that, repeat,
Cuckoo, bird, and open ear wells, heart-springs,
    delightfully sweet,
With a ballad, with a ballad, a rebound
Off trundled timber and scoops of the hillside ground,
    hollow hollow hollow ground:
The whole landscape flushes on a sudden at a sound.

England, 19th century

Kobayashi Issa

The snow thaws—
And suddenly the whole village
Is full of children!

Japan, 19th century
Trans. Lewis Mackenzie

from The Georgics
Book II, lines 328–345

Virgil

Then are the trackless copses alive with the trilling of birds,
And the beasts look for love, their hour come round again:
Lovely the earth in labour, under a tremulous west wind
The fields unbosom, a mild moisture is everywhere.
Confident grows the grass, for the young sun will not harm it;
The shoots of the vine are not scared of a southerly gale arising
Or the sleety rain that slants from heaven beneath a north wind,—

11

No, bravely now they bud and all their leaves display.
So it was, I believe, when the world first began,
Such the illustrious dawning and tenor of their days.
It was springtime then, great spring
Enhanced the earth and spared it the bitter breath of an east wind—
A time when the first cattle lapped up the light, and men
Children of earth themselves arose from the raw champaign,
And wild things issued forth in the wood, and stars in the sky.
How could so delicate creatures endure the toil they must,
Unless between cold and heat there came this temperate spell
And heaven held the earth in his arms and comforted her?

Italy, 1st century B.C.
Trans. from the Latin
by C. Day Lewis

The Thrush's Nest
John Clare

Within a thick and spreading hawthorn bush,
   That overhung a molehill large and round,
I heard from morn to morn a merry thrush
   Sing hymns to sunrise, and I drank the sound
With joy; and, often an intruding guest,
   I watched her secret toils from day to day—
How true she warped the moss to form a nest,
   And modelled it within with wood and clay;
And by and by, like heath-bells gilt with dew,
   There lay her shining eggs, as bright as flowers,
Ink-spotted-over shells of greeny blue;
   And there I witnessed in the sunny hours
A brood of nature's minstrels chirp and fly,
Glad as that sunshine and the laughing sky.

England, 19th century

Loveliest of trees, the cherry now
Is hung with bloom along the bough,
And stands about the woodland ride
Wearing white for Eastertide.

Now, of my threescore years and ten,
Twenty will not come again,
And take from seventy springs a score,
It only leaves me fifty more.

And since to look at things in bloom
Fifty springs are little room,
About the woodlands I will go
To see the cherry hung with snow.

England, 20th century

April Rise

Laurie Lee

If ever I saw blessing in the air
    I see it now in this still early day
Where lemon-green the vaporous morning drips
    Wet sunlight on the powder of my eye.

Blown bubble-film of blue, the sky wraps round
    Weeds of warm light whose every root and rod
Splutters with soapy green, and all the world
    Sweats with the bead of summer in its bud.

If ever I heard blessing it is there
    Where birds in trees that shoals and shadows are
Splash with their hidden wings, and drops of sound
    Break on my ears their crests of throbbing air.

Pure in the haze the emerald sun dilates,
   The lips of mosses milk the spongy stones,
While white as water by the lake a girl
   Swims her green hand among the gathered swans.

Now, as the almond burns its smoking wick,
   Dropping small flames to light the candled grass;
Now, as my low blood scales its second chance,
   If ever world were blessed, now it is.

England, 20th century

Butterflies

Chu Miao Tuan

The blossoms fall like snowflakes
On the cool, deep, dark-green moss,
They lie in white-heaped fragrant drifts
Before the courtyard gates.

The butterflies, not knowing
That the days of spring are done,
Still pursue the flying petals
Across the garden wall.

China, 18th century
Trans. Henry H. Hart

Image from D'Orleans

Ezra Pound

Young men riding in the street
In the bright new season
Spur without reason,
Causing their steeds to leap.

And at the pace they keep
Their horses' armoured feet
Strike sparks from the cobbled street
In the bright new season.

U.S.A., *20th century*

from The Canterbury Tales

Geoffrey Chaucer

THE PROLOGUE

When the sweet showers of April fall and shoot
Down through the drought of March to pierce the root,
Bathing every vein in liquid power
From which there springs the engendering of the flower,
When also Zephyrus with his sweet breath
Exhales an air in every grove and heath
Upon the tender shoots, and the young sun
His half-course in the sign of the *Ram* has run,
And the small fowl are making melody
That sleep away the night with open eye
(So nature pricks them and their heart engages)
Then people long to go on pilgrimages
And palmers long to seek the stranger strands
Of far-off saints, hallowed in sundry lands,
And specially, from every shire's end
In England, down to Canterbury they wend
To seek the holy blissful martyr, quick
In giving help to them when they were sick.
    It happened in that season that one day
In Southwark, at *The Tabard*, as I lay
Ready to go on pilgrimage and start
For Canterbury, most devout at heart,
At night there came into that hostelry
Some nine and twenty in a company
Of sundry folk happening then to fall
In fellowship, and they were pilgrims all
That towards Canterbury meant to ride.
The rooms and stables of the inn were wide;
They made us easy, all was of the best.
And shortly, when the sun had gone to rest,

from The Canterbury Tales

Geoffrey Chaucer

THE PROLOGUE

Here bygynneth the Book of the Tales of Caunterbury

Whan that Aprill with his shoures soote
The droghte of March hath perced to the roote,
And bathed every veyne in swich licour
Of which vertu engendred is the flour;
Whan Zephirus eek with his sweete breeth
Inspired hath in every holt and heeth
The tendre croppes, and the yonge sonne
Hath in the Ram his halve cours yronne,
And smale foweles maken melodye,
That slepen al the nyght with open ye,
(So priketh hem nature in hir corages);
Thanne longen folk to goon on pilgrimages
And palmeres for to seken straunge strondes
To ferne halwes, kowthe in sondry londes;
And specially from every shires ende
Of Engelond to Caunterbury they wende,
The hooly blisful martir for to seke,
That hem hath holpen whan that they were seeke.
   Bifil that, in that seson on a day,
In Southwerk at the Tabard as I lay
Redy to wenden on my pilgrymage
To Caunterbury with ful devout corage,
At nyght was come into that hostelrye
Wel nyne and twenty in a compaignye,
Of sondry folk, by aventure yfalle
In felaweshipe, and pilgrimes were they alle,
That toward Caunterbury wolden ryde;
The chambres and the stables weren wyde,
And wel we weren esed atte beste.
And shortly, whan the sonne was to reste,

By speaking to them all upon the trip
I was admitted to their fellowship
And promised to rise early and take the way
To Canterbury, as you heard me say.

But none the less, while I have time and space,
Before my story takes a further pace,
It seems a reasonable thing to say
What their condition was, the full array
Of each of them, as it appeared to me,
According to profession and degree,
And what apparel they were riding in;
And at a Knight I therefore will begin.

There was a *Knight*, a most distinguished man,
Who from the day on which he first began
To ride abroad had followed chivalry,
Truth, honour, generous thought and courtesy.
He had done nobly in his sovereign's war
And ridden into battle, no man more,
As well in christian as in heathen places,
And ever honoured for his noble graces. . . .
In fifteen mortal battles he had been
And jousted for our faith at Tramissene
Thrice in the lists, and always killed his man.
This same distinguished knight had led the van
Once with the Bey of Balat, doing work
For him against another heathen Turk;
He was of sovereign value in all eyes.
And though so much distinguished, he was wise
And in his bearing modest as a maid.
He never yet a boorish thing had said
In all his life to any, come what might;
He was a true, a perfect gentle-knight.
Speaking of his appearance, he possessed
Fine horses, but he was not gaily dressed.

So hadde I spoken with hem everichon
That I was of hir felaweshipe anon,
And made forward erly for to ryse,
To take oure wey ther as I yow devyse.

   But nathelees, whil I have tyme and space,
Er that I ferther in this tale pace,
Me thynketh it acordaunt to resoun
To telle yow al the condicioun
Of ech of hem, so as it semed me,
And whiche they weren, and of what degree,
And eek in what array that they were inne;
And at a knyght than wol I first bigynne.

   A *Knyght* ther was, and that a worthy man,
That fro the tyme that he first bigan
To riden out, he loved chivalrie,
Trouthe and honour, fredom and curteisie.
Ful worthy was he in his lordes werre,
And therto hadde he riden, no man ferre,
As wel in cristendom as hethenesse,
And evere honoured for his worthynesse. . . .
At mortal batailles hadde he been fiftene,
And foughten for oure feith at Tramyssene
In lystes thries, and ay slayn his foo.
This ilke worthy knyght hadde been also
Somtyme with the lord of Palatye,
Agayn another hethen in Turkye:
And everemoore he hadde a sovereyn prys;
And though that he were worthy, he was wys,
And of his port as meeke as is a mayde.
He nevere yet no vileynye ne sayde
In al his lyf, unto no maner wight.
He was a verray, parfit gentil knyght.
But, for to tellen yow of his array,
His hors were goode, but he was nat gay.

He wore a fustian tunic stained and dark
With smudges where his armour had left mark;
Just home from service, he had joined our ranks
To do his pilgrimage and render thanks.

He had his son with him, a fine young *Squire*,
A lover and cadet, a lad of fire
With curly locks, as if they had been pressed.
He was some twenty years of age, I guessed.
In stature he was of a moderate length,
With wonderful agility and strength.
He'd seen some service with the cavalry
In Flanders and Artois and Picardy
And had done valiantly in little space
Of time, in hope to win his lady's grace.
He was embroidered like a meadow bright
And full of freshest flowers, red and white.
Singing he was, or fluting all the day;
He was as fresh as is the month of May.
Short was his gown, the sleeves were long and wide;
He knew the way to sit a horse and ride.
He could make songs and poems and recite,
Knew how to joust and dance, to draw and write.
He loved so hotly that till dawn grew pale
He slept as little as a nightingale.
Courteous he was, lowly and serviceable,
And carved to serve his father at the table. . . .

There also was a *Nun*, a Prioress;
Simple her way of smiling was and coy.
Her greatest oath was only 'By St Loy!'
And she was known as Madam Eglantyne.
And well she sang a service, with a fine
Intoning through her nose, as was most seemly,
And she spoke daintily in French, extremely,
After the school of Stratford-atte-Bowe;

Of fustian he wered a gypon
Al bismotered with his habergeon,
For he was late ycome from his viage,
And wente for to doon his pilgrymage.

   With hym ther was his sone, a yong *Squier*,
A lovyere and a lusty bacheler,
With lokkes crulle as they were leyd in presse.
Of twenty yeer of age he was, I gesse.
Of his stature he was of evene lengthe,
And wonderly delyvere, and of greet strengthe.
And he hadde been somtyme in chyvachie,
In Flaundres, in Artoys, and Pycardie,
And born hym weel, as of so litel space,
In hope to stonden in his lady grace.
Embrouded was he, as it were a meede
Al ful of fresshe floures, whyte and reede.
Syngynge he was, or floytynge, al the day;
He was as fressh as is the month of May.
Short was his gowne, with sleves longe and wyde.
Wel koude he sitte on hors and faire ryde.
He koude songes make and wel endite,
Juste and eek daunce, and weel purtreye and write.
So hoote he lovede that by nyghtertale
He sleep namoore than dooth a nyghtyngale.
Curteis he was, lowely, and servysable,
And carf biforn his fader at the table. . . .

   Ther was also a *Nonne*, a Prioresse,
That of hir smylyng was ful symple and coy;
Hire gretteste ooth was but by Seinte Loy;
And she was cleped madame Eglentyne.
Ful weel she soong the service dyvyne,
Entuned in hir nose ful semely,
And Frenssh she spak ful faire and fetisly,
After the scole of Stratford atte Bowe,

French in the Paris style she did not know.
At meat her manners were well taught withal;
No morsel from her lips did she let fall,
Nor dipped her fingers in the sauce too deep;
But she could carry a morsel up and keep
The smallest drop from falling on her breast.
For courtliness she had a special zest.
And she would wipe her upper lip so clean
That not a trace of grease was to be seen
Upon the cup when she had drunk; to eat,
She reached a hand sedately for the meat. . . .
As for her sympathies and tender feelings,
She was so charitably solicitous
She used to weep if she but saw a mouse
Caught in a trap, if it were dead or bleeding.
And she had little dogs she would be feeding
With roasted flesh, or milk, or fine white bread.
Sorely she wept if one of them were dead
Or someone took a stick and made it smart;
She was all sentiment and tender heart. . . .
   Another *Nun*, the chaplain at her cell,
Was riding with her, and *three Priests* as well.

   There was a *Monk*, a leader of the fashions;
Inspecting farms and hunting were his passions,
Fit to be Abbot, a manly man and able.
Many the dainty horses in his stable;
His bridle, when he rode, a man might hear
Jingling in a whistling wind as clear,
Aye, and as loud as does the chapel bell
Where my lord Monk was Prior of the cell. . . .
Greyhounds he had, as swift as birds, to course.
Hunting a hare or riding at a fence
Was all his fun, he spared for no expense.
I saw his sleeves were garnished at the hand
With fine grey fur, the finest in the land,

For Frenssh of Parys was to hire unknowe.
At mete wel ytaught was she with alle;
She leet no morsel from hir lippes falle,
Ne wette hir fyngres in hir sauce depe;
Wel koude she carie a morsel and wel kepe
That no drope ne fille upon hire brest.
In curteisie was set ful muchel hir lest.
Hir over-lippe wyped she so clene
That in hir coppe was no ferthyng sene
Of grece, whan she dronken hadde hir draughte.
Ful semely after hir mete she raughte. . . .
But, for to speken of hir conscience,
She was so charitable and so pitous
She wolde wepe, if that she saugh a mous
Kaught in a trappe, if it were deed or bledde.
Of smale houndes hadde she that she fedde
With rosted flessh, or milk and wastel-breed.
But sore wepte she if oon of hem were deed,
Or if men smoot it with a yerde smerte:
And al was conscience and tendre herte. . . .
   Another *Nonne* with hire hadde she,
That was hir chapeleyne, and *Preestes* thre.

   A *Monk* ther was, a fair for the maistrie,
An outridere, that lovede venerie;
A manly man, to been an abbot able.
Ful many a deyntee hors hadde he in stable,
And whan he rood, men myghte his brydel heere
Gynglen in a whistlynge wynd als cleere,
And eek as loude as dooth the chapel belle,
Ther as this lord was keper of the celle. . . .
Grehoundes he hadde as swift as fowel in flight;
Of prikyng and of hunting for the hare
Was al his lust, for no cost wolde he spare.
I seigh his sleves purfiled at the hond
With grys, and that of the fyneste of a lond;

And where his hood was fastened at his chin
He had a wrought-gold cunningly fashioned pin;
Into a lover's knot it seemed to pass.
His head was bald and shone as any glass,
So did his face, as if it had been greased.
He was a fat and personable priest;
His bright eyes rolled, they never seemed to settle,
And glittered like the flames beneath a kettle;
Supple his boots, his horse in fine condition.
He was a prelate fit for exhibition,
He was not pale like a tormented soul.
He liked a fat swan best, and roasted whole.
His palfrey was as brown as is a berry. . .

A land-owner, a *Franklin*, had appeared;
White as a daisy-petal was his beard.
A sanguine man, high-coloured and benign,
He loved a morning sop of cake in wine.
He lived for pleasure and had always done,
For he was Epicurus' very son,
In whose opinion sensual delight
Was the one true felicity in sight. . . .
His house was never short of bake-meat pies,
Of fish and flesh, and these in such supplies
It positively snowed with meat and drink
And all the dainties that a man could think.
According to the seasons of the year
Changes of dish were ordered to appear.
He kept fat partridges in coops, beyond,
Many a bream and pike were in his pond. . . .

They had a *Cook* with them who stood alone
For boiling chicken with a marrow-bone,
Sharp flavouring-powder and a spice for savour.
He could distinguish London ale by flavour,
And he could roast and seethe and broil and fry,

And, for to festne his hood under his chyn,
He hadde of gold ywroght a ful curious pyn;
A love-knotte in the gretter ende ther was.
His heed was balled, that shoon as any glas,
And eek his face, as he hadde been enoynt.
He was a lord ful fat and in good poynt;
His eyen stepe, and rollynge in his heed,
That stemed as a forneys of a leed;
His bootes souple, his hors in greet estaat.
Now certeinly he was a fair prelaat;
He was nat pale as a forpyned goost.
A fat swan loved he best of any roost.
His palfrey was as broun as is a berye. . . .

A *Frankeleyn* was in his compaignye;
Whit was his berd as is the dayesye.
Of his complexioun he was sangwyn.
Wel loved he by the morwe a sop in wyn;
To lyven in delit was evere his wone,
For he was Epicurus owene sone,
That heeld opinioun that pleyn delit
Was verraily felicitee parfit. . . .
Withoute bake mete was nevere his hous
Of fissh and flessh, and that so plentevous,
It snewed in his hous of mete and drynke,
Of alle deyntees that men koude thynke.
After the sondry sesons of the yeer,
So chaunged he his mete and his soper.
Ful many a fat partrich hadde he in muwe,
And many a breem and many a luce in stuwe. . . .

A *Cook* they hadde with hem for the nones
To boille the chiknes with the marybones,
And poudre-marchant tart and galyngale.
Wel koude he knowe a draughte of Londoun ale.
He koude rooste, and sethe, and broille, and frye,

25

Make good thick soup and bake a tasty pie.
But a great pity, as it seemed to me,
Was that he had a gangrene on his knee.
As for blancmange, he made it with the best.

There was a *Skipper* hailing from far west;
He came from Dartmouth, so I understood.
He rode a farmer's horse as best he could,
In a woollen gown that reached his knee.
A dagger on a lanyard falling free
Hung from his neck under his arm and down.
The summer heat had tanned his colour brown,
And certainly he was an excellent fellow.
Many a draught of vintage, red and yellow,
He'd drawn at Bordeaux, while the vintner slept.
Few were the rules his tender conscience kept.
If, when he fought, the enemy vessel sank,
He sent his prisoners home; they walked the plank.
As for his skill in reckoning his tides,
Currents and many another risk besides,
Moons, harbours, pilots, he had such dispatch
That none from Hull to Carthage was his match.
Hardy he was, prudent in undertaking;
His beard in many a tempest had its shaking,
And he knew all the havens as they were
From Gottland to the Cape of Finisterre,
And every creek in Brittany and Spain;
The barge he owned was called *The Maudelayne*.

A *Doctor* too emerged as we proceeded;
No one alive could talk as well as he did
On points of medicine and of surgery,
For, being grounded in astronomy,
He watched his patient's favourable star
And, by his Natural Magic, knew what are
The lucky hours and planetary degrees

26

Maken mortreux, and wel bake a pye.
But greet harm was it, as it thoughte me,
That on his shyne a mormal hadde he.
For blankmanger, that made he with the beste.

A *Shipman* was ther, wonynge fer by weste;
For aught I woot, he was of Dertemouthe.
He rood upon a rouncy, as he kouthe,
In a gowne of faldyng to the knee.
A daggere hangynge on a laas hadde he
Aboute his nekke, under his arm adoun.
The hoote somer hadde maad his hewe al broun;
And certeinly he was a good felawe.
Ful many a draughte of wyn had he ydrawe
Fro Burdeux-ward, whil that the chapman sleep.
Of nyce conscience took he no keep.
If that he faught, and hadde the hyer hond,
By water he sente hem hoom to every lond.
But of his craft to rekene wel his tydes,
His stremes, and his daungers hym bisydes,
His herberwe, and his moone, his lodemenage,
Ther nas noon swich from Hulle to Cartage.
Hardy he was and wys to undertake;
With many a tempest hadde his berd been shake.
He knew alle the havenes, as they were,
Fro Gootlond to the cape of Fynystere,
And every cryke in Britaigne and in Spayne;
His barge ycleped was the Maudelayne.

With us ther was a *Doctour of Phisik*,
In al this world ne was ther noon hym lik
To speke of phisik and of surgerye,
For he was grounded in astronomye.
He kepte his pacient a ful greet deel
In houres by his magyk natureel.
Wel koude he fortunen the ascendent

27

For making charms and magic effigies.
The cause of every malady you'd got
He knew, and whether dry, cold, moist or hot;
He knew their seat, their humour and condition.
He was a perfect practising physician. . . .

A worthy *woman* from beside *Bath* city
Was with us, somewhat deaf, which was a pity.
In making cloth she showed so great a bent
She bettered those of Ypres and of Ghent.
In all the parish not a dame dared stir
Towards the altar steps in front of her,
And if indeed they did, so wrath was she
As to be quite put out of charity.
Her kerchiefs were of finely woven ground;
I dared have sworn they weighed a good ten pound,
The ones she wore on Sunday, on her head.
Her hose were of the finest scarlet red
And gartered tight; her shoes were soft and new.
Bold was her face, handsome, and red in hue.
A worthy woman all her life, what's more
She'd had five husbands, all at the church door,
Apart from other company in youth;
No need just now to speak of that, forsooth. . . .
And she was skilled in wandering by the way.
She had gap-teeth, set widely, truth to say.
Easily on an ambling horse she sat
Well wimpled up, and on her head a hat
As broad as is a buckler or a shield;
She had a flowing mantle that concealed
Large hips, her heels spurred sharply under that.
In company she liked to laugh and chat. . . .

A holy-minded man of good renown
There was, and poor, the *Parson* to a town,
Yet he was rich in holy thought and work.

Of his ymages for his pacient.
He knew the cause of everich maladye,
Were it of hoot, or coold, or moyste, or drye,
And where they engendred, and of what humour.
He was a verray, parfit praktisour. . . .

A good *Wif* was ther *of* biside *Bathe*,
But she was somdel deef, and that was scathe.
Of clooth-makyng she hadde swich an haunt,
She passed hem of Ypres and of Gaunt.
In al the parisshe wif ne was ther noon
That to the offrynge bifore hire sholde goon;
And if ther dide, certeyn so wrooth was she,
That she was out of alle charitee.
Hir coverchiefs ful fyne weren of ground;
I dorste swere they weyeden ten pound
That on a Sonday weren upon hir heed.
Hir hosen weren of fyn scarlet reed,
Ful streite yteyd, and shoes ful moyste and newe.
Boold was hir face, and fair, and reed of hewe.
She was a worthy womman al hir lyve:
Housbondes at chirche dore she hadde fyve,
Withouten oother compaignye in youthe;
But therof nedeth nat to speke as nowthe. . . .
She koude muchel of wandrynge by the weye.
Gat-tothed was she, soothly for to seye.
Upon an amblere esily she sat,
Ywympled wel, and on hir heed an hat
As brood as is a bokeler or a targe;
A foot-mantel aboute hir hipes large,
And on hir feet a paire of spores sharpe.
In felaweshipe wel koude she laughe and carpe. . . .

A good man was ther of religioun,
And was a povre *Persoun* of a toun;
But riche he was of hooly thoght and werk.

He also was a learned man, a clerk,
Who truly knew Christ's gospel and would preach it
Devoutly to parishioners, and teach it.
Benign and wonderfully diligent,
And patient when adversity was sent . . .
Wide was his parish, with houses far asunder,
Yet he neglected not in rain or thunder,
In sickness or in grief, to pay a call
On the remotest whether great or small
Upon his feet, and in his hand a stave.
This noble example to his sheep he gave,
First following the word before he taught it,
And it was from the gospel he had caught it.
This little proverb he would add thereto
That if gold rust, what then will iron do? . . .
I think there never was a better priest.
He sought no pomp or glory in his dealings,
No scrupulosity had spiced his feelings.
Christ and His Twelve Apostles and their lore
He taught, but followed it himself before. . . .

The *Miller* was a chap of sixteen stone,
A great stout fellow big in brawn and bone.
He did well out of them, for he could go
And win the ram at any wrestling show.
Broad, knotty and short-shouldered, he would boast
He could heave any door off hinge and post,
Or take a run and break it with his head.
His beard, like any sow or fox, was red
And broad as well, as though it were a spade;
And, at its very tip, his nose displayed
A wart on which there stood a tuft of hair
Red as the bristles in an old sow's ear.
His nostrils were as black as they were wide,
He had a sword and buckler at his side,
His mighty mouth was like a furnace door.

He was also a lerned man, a clerk,
That Cristes gospel trewely wolde preche;
His parisshens devoutly wolde he teche.
Benygne he was, and wonder diligent,
And in adversitee ful pacient . . .
Wyd was his parisshe, and houses fer asonder,
But he ne lefte nat, for reyn ne thonder,
In siknesse nor in meschief, to visite
The ferreste in his parisshe, muche and lite,
Upon his feet, and in his hand a staf.
This noble ensample to his sheep he yaf,
That first he wroghte, and afterward he taughte.
Out of the gospel he tho wordes caughte,
And this figure he added eek therto,
That if gold ruste, what shal iren do? . . .
A bettre preest I trowe that nowher noon ys.
He waited after no pompe and reverence,
Ne maked him a spiced conscience,
But Cristes loore, and his apostles twelve
He taughte, and first he folwed it hymselve. . . .

The *Millere* was a stout carl for the nones;
Ful byg he was of brawn, and eek of bones.
That proved wel, for over al ther he cam,
At wrastlynge he wolde have alwey the ram.
He was short-sholdred, brood, a thikke knarre;
Ther was no dore that he nolde heve of harre,
Or breke it at a rennyng with his heed.
His berd as any sowe or fox was reed,
And therto brood, as though it were a spade.
Upon the cop right of his nose he hade
A werte, and theron stood a toft of herys,
Reed as the brustles of a sowes erys;
His nosethirles blake were and wyde.
A swerd and bokeler bar he by his syde.
His mouth as greet was as a greet forneys.

31

A wrangler and buffoon, he had a store
Of tavern stories, filthy in the main.
His was a master-hand at stealing grain.
He felt it with his thumb and thus he knew
Its quality and took three times his due—
A thumb of gold, by God, to gauge an oat!
He wore a hood of blue and a white coat.
He liked to play his bagpipes up and down
And that was how he brought us out of town.

England, 14th century
Trans. Nevill Coghill

He was a janglere and a goliardeys,
And that was moost of sinne and harlotries.
Wel koude he stelen corn, and tollen thries;
And yet he hadde a thombe of gold, pardee.

A whit cote and a blew hood wered he.
A baggepipe wel koude he blowe and sowne,
And therwithal he broghte us out of towne.

England, 14th century

Chiyo-Ni

Spring rain:
Everything just grows
More beautiful.

Japan, 18th century
Trans. R. H. Blyth

Cuccu Song

Anon.

Sumer is icumen in;
    Lhude sing cuccu!
Groweth sed, and bloweth med,
    And springeth the wude nu.
        Sing cuccu!

Awe bleteth after lomb,
    Lhouth after calve cu;
Bulluc sterteth, bucke verteth,
    Murie sing cuccu!

Cuccu, cuccu, well singes thu, cuccu:
    Ne swike thu naver nu:
Sing cuccu, nu, sing cuccu,
    Sing cuccu, sing cuccu, nu!

England, 13th century

Chamber Music (XXXV)

James Joyce

All day I hear the noise of waters
        Making moan,
Sad as the seabird is when going
        Forth alone
He hears the winds cry to the waters'
        Monotone.

34

The grey winds, the cold winds are blowing
    Where I go.
I hear the noise of many waters
    Far below.
All day, all night, I hear them flowing
    To and fro.

Ireland, 20th century

A Storm in Childhood

T. H. Jones

We had taken the long way home, a mile
Or two further than any of us had to walk,
But it meant being together longer, and home later.

The storm broke on us—broke is a cliché,
But us isn't—that storm was loosed for us, on us.
My cousin Blodwen, oldest and wisest of us,
Said in a voice we'd never heard her use before:
'The lightning kills you when it strikes the trees.'
If we were in anything besides a storm, it was trees.
On our left, the valley bottom was nothing but trees,
And on our right the trees went halfway up
The hill. We ran, between the trees and the trees,
Five children hand-in-hand, afraid of God,
Afraid of being among the lightning-fetching
Trees, soaked, soaked with rain, with sweat, with tears,
Frightened, if that's the adequate word, frightened
By the loud voice and the lambent threat,
Frightened certainly of whippings for being late,
Five children, ages six to eleven, stumbling
After a bit of running through trees from God.
Even my cousin who was eleven—I can't remember
If she was crying, too—I suppose I hope so.
But I do remember the younger ones when the stumbling
Got worse as the older terror of trees got worse

35

Adding their tears' irritation to the loud world of wet
And tall trees waiting to be struck by the flash, and us
With them—that running stumble, hand-in-hand—five
Children aware of our sins as we ran stumblingly:
Our sins which seemed such pointless things to talk
About to mild Miss Davies on the hard Sunday benches.

The lightning struck no trees, nor any of us.
I think we all got beaten; some of us got colds.
It was the longest race I ever ran,
A race against God's voice sounding from the hills
And his blaze aimed at the trees and at us,
A race in the unfriendly rain, with only the other
Children, hand-in-hand, to comfort me to know
They too were frightened, all of us miserable sinners.

Wales, 20th century

from Resolution and Independence
William Wordsworth

There was a roaring in the wind all night;
The rain came heavily and fell in floods;
But now the sun is rising calm and bright;
The birds are singing in the distant woods;
Over his own sweet voice the stock-dove broods;
The jay makes answer as the magpie chatters;
And all the air is filled with pleasant noise of waters.

All things that love the sun are out of doors;
The sky rejoices in the morning's birth;
The grass is bright with rain-drops;—on the moors
The hare is running races in her mirth;
And with her feet she from the plashy earth
Raises a mist, that glittering in the sun,
Runs with her all the way, wherever she doth run.

England, 19th century

Wind

Ted Hughes

This house has been far out at sea all night,
The woods crashing through darkness, the booming hills,
Winds stampeding the fields under the window
Floundering black astride and blinding wet

Till day rose; then under an orange sky
The hills had new places, and wind wielded
Blade-like, luminous black and emerald,
Flexing like the lens of a mad eye.

At noon I scaled along the house-side as far as
The coal-house door. I dared once to look up—
Through the brunt wind that dented the balls of my eyes
The tent of the hills drummed and strained its guyrope,

The fields quivering, the skyline a grimace,
At any second to bang and vanish with a flap:
The wind flung a magpie away and a black-
Back gull bent like an iron bar slowly. The house

Rang like some fine green goblet in the note
That any second would shatter it. Now deep
In chairs, in front of the great fire, we grip
Our hearts and cannot entertain book, thought,

Or each other. We watch the fire blazing,
And feel the roots of the house move, but sit on,
Seeing the window tremble to come in,
Hearing the stones cry out under the horizons.

England, 20th century

The History of the Flood

John Heath-Stubbs

Bang Bang Bang
Said the nails in the Ark.

It's getting rather dark
Said the nails in the Ark.

For the rain is coming down
Said the nails in the Ark.

And you're all like to drown
Said the nails in the Ark.

Dark and black as sin
Said the nails in the Ark.

So won't you all come in
Said the nails in the Ark.

But only two by two
Said the nails in the Ark.

So they come in two by two,
The elephant, the kangaroo,
And the gnu,
And the little tiny shrew.

Then the birds
Flocked in like wingèd words:
Two racket-tailed motmots, two macaws,
Two nuthatches and two
Little bright robins.

And the reptiles: the gila monster, the slow-worm,
The green mamba, the cottonmouth, and the alli-
        gator—
All squirmed in;
And after a very lengthy walk,
Two giant Galapagos tortoises.

And the insects in their hierarchies:
A queen ant, a king ant, a queen wasp, a king wasp,
A queen bee, a king bee,
And all the beetles, bugs and mosquitoes,
Cascaded in like glittering, murmurous jewels.

But the fish had their wish;
For the rain came down.
People began to drown:
The wicked, the rich—
They gasped out bubbles of pure gold,
Which exhalations
Rose to the constellations.

So for forty days and forty nights
They were on the waste of waters
In those cramped quarters.
It was very dark, damp and lonely.
There was nothing to see, but only
The rain which continued to drop.
It did not stop.

So Noah sent forth a Raven. The raven said 'Kark!
I will not go back to the ark.'
The raven was footloose,
He fed on the bodies of the rich—
Rich with vitamins and goo.
They had become bloated,
And everywhere they floated.
The raven's heart was black,

He did not come back.
It was not a nice thing to do:
Which is why the raven is a token of wrath,
And creaks like a rusty gate
When he crosses your path; and Fate
Will grant you no luck that day:
The raven is fey:
You were meant to have a scare.
Fortunately in England
The raven is rather rare.

Then Noah sent forth a dove
She did not want to rove.
She longed for her love—
The other turtle dove—
(For her no other dove!)
She brought back a twig from an olive-tree.
There is no more beautiful tree
Anywhere on the earth,
Even when it comes to birth
From six weeks under the sea.

She did not want to rove.
She wanted to take her rest,
And to build herself a nest
All in the olive grove.
She wanted to make love.
She thought that was the best.

The dove was not a rover;
So they knew that the rain was over.
Noah and his wife got out
(They had become rather stout)
And Japhet, Ham, and Shem.
(The same could be said of them.)
They looked up at the sky.
The earth was becoming dry.

Then the animals came ashore—
There were more of them than before:
There were two dogs and a litter of puppies;
There were a tom-cat and two tib-cats
And two litters of kittens—cats
Do not obey regulations;
And, as you might expect,
A quantity of rabbits.

God put a rainbow in the sky.
They wondered what it was for.
There had never been a rainbow before.
The rainbow was a sign;
It looked like a neon sign—
Seven colours arched in the skies:
What should it publicise?
They looked up with wondering eyes.

It advertises Mercy
Said the nails in the Ark.

Mercy Mercy Mercy
Said the nails in the Ark.

Our God is merciful
Said the nails in the Ark.

Merciful and gracious
Bang Bang Bang Bang.

England, 20th century

Such is Holland!

Petrus Augustus de Genestet

O, land of mud and mist, where man is wet and shivers
   Soaked with humidity, with damp and chilly dew,
    O, land of unplumbed bogs, of roads resembling rivers,
Land of umbrellas, gout, colds, agues, toothache, flu,

O, spongy porridge-swamp, O homeland of galoshes,
   Of cobblers, toads, and frogs, peat diggers, mildew, mould,
Of ducks and every bird that slobbers, splutters, splashes,
   Hear the autumnal plaint of a poet with a cold.

Thanks to your clammy clime my arteries are clotted
   With blood turned mud. No song, no joy, no peace for me.
   You're fit for clogs alone, O land our forebears plotted
And, not at my request, extorted from the sea.

Netherlands, 19th century
Trans. Adriaan J. Barnouw

Ariel's Song *from* The Tempest

William Shakespeare

Full fathom five thy father lies;
   Of his bones are coral made;
Those are pearls that were his eyes:
   Nothing of him that doth fade,
But doth suffer a sea-change
Into something rich and strange.
Sea-nymphs hourly ring his knell:
             Ding-dong.
Hark now I hear them, ding–dong bell.

England, 16th century

Old Deep Sing-Song

Carl Sandburg

in the old deep sing-song of the sea
in the old going-on of that sing-song
in that old mama-mama-mama going-on
of that nightlong daylong sleepsong
we look on   we listen
we lay by and hear
too many big bells   too many long gongs
too many weepers over a lost gone gold
too many laughs over light green gold
woven and changing in the wash and the heave
moving on the bottoms   winding in the waters
sending themselves with arms and voices
up in the old mama-mama-mama music
up into the whirl of spokes of light

U.S.A., 20th century

The Shell

James Stephens

And then I pressed the shell
Close to my ear
And listened well.
And straightway, like a bell,
Came low and clear
The slow, sad murmur of far distant seas
Whipped by an icy breeze
Upon a shore
Wind-swept and desolate.
It was a sunless strand that never bore
The footprint of a man,
Nor felt the weight
Since time began
Of any human quality or stir,
Save what the dreary winds and waves incur.

43

And in the hush of waters was the sound
Of pebbles, rolling round;
For ever rolling, with a hollow sound:
And bubbling sea-weeds as the waters go,
Swish to and fro
Their long cold tentacles of slimy grey.
There was no day;
Nor ever came a night
Setting the stars alight
To wonder at the moon:
Was twilight only, and the frightened croon,
Smitten to whimpers, of the dreary wind
And waves that journeyed blind . . .
And then I loosed my ear—Oh, it was sweet
To hear a cart go jolting down the street.

Ireland, 20th century

On This Island

W. H. Auden

Look, stranger, on this island now
The leaping light for your delight discovers,
Stand stable here
And silent be,
That through the channels of the ear
May wander like a river
The swaying sound of the sea.

Here at the small field's ending pause
When the chalk wall falls to the foam and its
    tall ledges
Oppose the pluck
And knock of the tide,
And the shingle scrambles after the suck-
    ing surf,
And a gull lodges
A moment on its sheer side.

Far off like floating seeds the ships
Diverge on urgent voluntary errands,
And this full view
Indeed may enter
And move in memory as now these clouds do,
That pass the harbour mirror
And all the summer through the water saunter.

U.S.A., *20th century*

from Beowulf's Voyage to Denmark

Anon.

He bade a seaworthy
wave-cutter be fitted out for him; the warrior king
he would seek, he said, over swan's riding,
that lord of name, needing men.

The wiser sought to dissuade him from voyaging
hardly or not at all, though they held him dear;
whetted his quest-thirst, watched omens.

The prince had already picked his men
from the folk's flower, the fiercest among them
that might be found. With fourteen men
sought sound-wood: sea-wise Beowulf
led them right down to the land's edge.

Time running on, she rode the waves now
hard in by headland. Harnessed warriors
stepped on her stem; setting tide churned
sea with sand, soldiers carried
bright mail-coats to the mast's foot,
war-gear well-wrought; willingly they shoved her out,
thorough-braced craft, on the craved voyage.

Away she went over a wavy ocean,
boat like a bird, breaking seas,
wind-whetted, white-throated,
till curved prow had ploughed so far
—the sun standing right on the second day—
that they might see land loom on the skyline,
then the shimmer of cliffs, sheer moors behind,
reaching capes.

England, 8th century
Trans. from the Anglo-
Saxon by Michael Alexander

Sir Patrick Spens

Anon.

The King sits in Dunferling toune,
Drinking the blude-red wine:
O quhar will I get guid sailor,
To sail this schip of mine?

Up and spak an eldern knicht,
Sat at the King's richt knee:
Sir Patrick Spens is the best sailor,
That sails upon the sea.

The King has written a braid letter,
And signed it wi' his hand;
And sent it to Sir Patrick Spens,
Was walking on the sand.

The first line that Sir Patrick red
A loud lauch lauched he:
The next line that Sir Patrick red
The teir blinded his ee.

O quha is this has done this deid,
This ill deid done to me;
To send me out this time o' the yeir,
To sail upon the sea?

The Return

Mak haste, mak haste, my mirry men all,
Our good schip sails the morne;
O say na sae, my master deir,
For I feir a deadlie storme.

Late late yestreen I saw the new moone
Wi' the auld moone in hir arme,
And I feir, I feir, my deir master,
That we will come to harme.

O our Scots nobles wer richt laith
To weet their cork-heild schoone,
But lang owre a' the play were played,
Their hats they swam aboone.

O lang, lang may their ladies sit
Wi' their fans into their hand,
Or e'er they see Sir Patrick Spens
Cum sailing to the land.

O lang, lang may the ladies stand
Wi' thair gold kems in their hair,
Waiting for their ain deir lords,
For they'll see thame ne mair.

Have owre, have owre to Aberdour,
It's fifty fadom deip;
And thair lies guid Sir Patrick Spens,
Wi' the Scots lords at his feit.

Scotland, trad.

from The Nightfishing

W. S. Graham

We are at the hauling then hoping for it
The hard slow haul of a net white with herring
Meshed hard. I haul, using the boat's cross-heave
We've started, holding fast as we rock back,
Taking slack as we go to. The day rises brighter
Over us and the gulls rise in a wailing scare
From the nearest net-floats. And the unfolding water
Mingles its dead.

Now better white I can say what's better sighted,
The white net flashing under the watched water,
The near net dragging back with the full belly
Of a good take certain, so drifted easy
Slow down on us or us hauled up upon it
Curved in a garment down to thicker fathoms.
The hauling nets come in sawing the gunwale
With herring scales.

The air bunches to a wind and roused sea-cries.
The weather moves and stoops high over us and
There the forked tern, where my look's whetted on
        distance,
Quarters its hunting sea. I haul slowly
Inboard the drowning flood as into memory,
Braced at the breathside in my net of nerves.
We haul and drift them home. The winds slowly
Turn round on us and

Gather towards us with dragging weights of water
Sleekly swelling across the humming sea
And gather heavier. We haul and hold and haul
Well the bright chirpers home, so drifted whitely

All a blinding garment out of the grey water.
And, hauling hard in the drag, the nets come in,
The head rope a sore pull and feeding its brine
Into our hacked hands.

Over the gunwale over into our deep lap
The herring come in, staring from their scales,
Fruitful as our deserts would have it out of
The deep and shifting seams of water. We haul
Against time fallen ill over the gathering
Rush of the sea together. The calms dive down.
The strident kingforked airs roar in their shell.
We haul the last

Net home and the last tether off the gathering
Run of the started sea. And then was the first
Hand at last lifted getting us swung against
Into the homing quarter, running that white grace
That sails me surely ever away from home.
And we hold into it as it moves down on
Us running white on the hull heeled to light.
Our bow heads home

Into the running blackbacks soaring us loud
High up in open arms of the towering sea.
The steep bow heaves, hung on these words, towards
What words your lonely breath blows out to meet it.
It is the skilled keel itself knowing its own
Fathoms it further moves through, with us there
Kept in its common timbers, yet each of us
Unwound upon

By a lonely behaviour of the all common ocean.

England, 20th century

49

The North Ship
Legend

Philip Larkin

I saw three ships go sailing by,
Over the sea, the lifting sea,
And the wind rose in the morning sky,
And one was rigged for a long journey.

The first ship turned towards the west,
Over the sea, the running sea,
And by the wind was all possessed
And carried to a rich country.

The second turned towards the east,
Over the sea, the quaking sea,
And the wind hunted it like a beast
To anchor in captivity.

The third ship drove towards the north,
Over the sea, the darkening sea,
But no breath of wind came forth,
And the decks shone frostily.

The northern sky rose high and black
Over the proud unfruitful sea,
East and west the ships came back
Happily or unhappily:

But the third went wide and far
Into an unforgiving sea
Under a fire-spilling star,
And it was rigged for a long journey.

England, 20th century

Dreams of a Summer Night, PART VI

THE CUTTY SARK

George Barker

I think of her where she lies there on her stone couch by the Thames
With the winds of the world asleep among her shrouds and the
    gales
Hushed in her furled sails and the pawing white sea horses
At last at rest around her and the mermen of yesterday calling to
    her
From the wind tossed reach of the river as it sweeps through
    Greenwich
Meridian. I think of her as I think of a seagull caged in chains but
Still standing poised, prepared, wings lifted, for the rise and veer
Into the sunrise of Asia as far as the paradise islands of
The Coral Sea. And all the great figureheads fraternising below
    her decks
Like Kings and queens at a feast—the *Cleopatra*, the *Lallah*
    Rookh,
Abraham Lincoln, Thermopylae, the *American Officer,*
Diana, and *Marianne,* filling her hold with the dialogues
Of storms and calms, of long summer days and seas
Whispering in their dreams, all join with the voices of
The dead sailor roped at the chained wheel and
The ghosts that lean singing into the bitter wind that drives
    up from
The thundering graves of the sea.

England, 20th century

The Yachts

William Carlos Williams

contend in a sea which the land partly encloses
shielding them from the too-heavy blows
of an ungoverned ocean which when it chooses

51

tortures the biggest hulls, the best man knows
to pit against its beatings, and sinks them pitilessly.
Mothlike in mists, scintillant in the minute

brilliance of cloudless days, with broad bellying sails
they glide to the wind tossing green water
from their sharp prows while over them the crew crawls

ant-like, solicitously grooming them, releasing,
making fast as they turn, lean far over and having
caught the wind again, side by side, head for the mark.

In a well guarded arena of open water surrounded by
lesser and greater craft which, sycophant, lumbering
and flittering follow them, they appear youthful, rare

as the light of a happy eye, live with the grace
of all that in the mind is fleckless, free and
naturally to be desired. Now the sea which holds them

is moody, lapping their glossy sides, as if feeling
for some slightest flaw but fails completely.
Today no race. Then the wind comes again. The yachts

move, jockeying for a start, the signal is set and they
are off. Now the waves strike at them but they are too
well made, they slip through, though they take in canvas.

Arms with hands grasping seek to clutch at the prows.
Bodies thrown recklessly in the way are cut aside.
It is a sea of faces about them in agony, in despair

until the horror of the race dawns staggering the mind,
the whole sea become an entanglement of watery bodies
lost to the world bearing what they cannot hold. Broken,

beaten, desolate, reaching from the dead to be taken up
they cry out, failing, failing! their cries rising
in waves still as the skilful yachts pass over.

U.S.A., 20th century

52

from Dover Beach

Matthew Arnold

The sea is calm tonight.
The tide is full, the moon lies fair
Upon the straits;—on the French coast the light
Gleams and is gone; the cliffs of England stand
Glimmering and vast, out in the tranquil bay.
Come to the window, sweet is the night-air!
Only, from the long line of spray
Where the sea meets the moon-blanched land,
Listen! You hear the grating roar
Of pebbles which the waves draw back, and fling,
At their return, up the high strand,
Begin, and cease, and then again begin,
With tremulous cadence slow, and bring
The eternal note of sadness in.

England, 19th century

Looking at the moon on putting out from the shore at Nagato

Anon.

Behind the mountain ledge
The moon creeps and hides;
The lights of the fishing-boats
Are mirrored over the open sea.

We think our boat is alone
Rowed through the black night:
Then from the open sea
Comes the plash of paddles.

Japan, 8th century
Trans. Bownas & Thwaite

Boats at Night

Edward Shanks

How lovely is the sound of oars at night
And unknown voices, borne through windless air,
From shadowy vessels floating out of sight
Beyond the harbour lantern's broken glare
To those piled rocks that make on the dark wave
Only a darker stain. The splashing oars
Slide softly on as in an echoing cave
And with the whisper of the unseen shores
Mingle their music, till the bell of night
Murmurs reverberations low and deep,
That droop towards the land in swooning flight
Like whispers from the lazy lips of sleep.
The oars grow faint. Below the cloud-dim hill
The shadows fade and now the bay is still.

England, 20th century

Uejima Onitsura

A trout leaps high—
Below him in the river bottom
Clouds flow by.

Japan, 17th century
Trans. Harold G. Henderson

Sonnet of Fishes

George Barker

Bright drips the morning from its trophied nets
Looped along a sky flickering fish and wing,
Cobbles like salmon crowd up waterfalling
Streets where life dies thrashing as the sea forgets,

True widow, what she has lost; and, ravished, lets
The knuckledustered sun shake bullying
A fist of glory over her. Everything,
Even the sly night, gives up its lunar secrets.

And I with pilchards cold in my pocket make
Red-eyed a way to bed. But in my blood
Crying I hear, still, the leap of the silver diver
Caught in four cords after his fatal strake;
And then, the immense imminence not understood,
Death, in a dark, in a deep, in a dream, forever.

England, 20th century

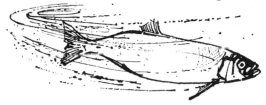

How to Catch Tiddlers

Brian Jones

Watch the net drift. Grey tides
Mingle what purposes your eye supposed
But watch the net. There is no fish
Only the net, the way it moves. There is no fish,
Forget the fish. The net is spread
And moving. Steer gently. Keep the hand
Pressured constantly against the stream.
There is no catch now, only the net
And your pressure and your poise. Below
Ignore the pebbles and the promising weed
Mooning over its secrets. There is just the net,

The hand, and, now, near an old glance
    somewhere
A sleek shape holding its body constant,
Firm in its fluid world. Move on. Watch
Only the net. You are a hand only,
Steering, controlling. Now look.
Inside that silent bulge the shape
Breaks black and firm. You may rise,
You may rise now—the deftest
Turn of the wrist will do it. Your hand
Crude again can support the cling of mesh.
You can relax, coldly note
The titchy black squirm. You have achieved.
Commit success to jamjars. Lean again.
Dip the slack net. Let it belly.

England, 20th century

Night Song of the Fish

Christian Morgenstern

Germany, 19th century

The Cat and the Moon

W. B. Yeats

The cat went here and there
And the moon spun round like a top,
And the nearest kin of the moon,
The creeping cat, looked up.
Black Minnaloushe stared at the moon,
For, wander and wail as he would,
The pure cold light in the sky
Troubled his animal blood.
Minnaloushe runs in the grass
Lifting his delicate feet.
Do you dance, Minnaloushe, do you dance?
When two close kindred meet,
What better than call a dance?
Maybe the moon may learn,
Tired of that courtly fashion,
A new dance turn.
Minnaloushe creeps through the grass
From moonlit place to place,
The sacred moon overhead
Has taken a new phase.
Does Minnaloushe know that his pupils
Will pass from change to change,
And that from round to crescent,
From crescent to round they range?
Minnaloushe creeps through the grass
Alone, important and wise,
And lifts to the changing moon
His changing eyes.

Ireland, 20th century

Cat in the Long Grass

Alan Dixon

Seeing the size, the domed
depth of a cat's ear, the sensitive
membrane furred over
with fine curls,
I am surprised he walks
a true wild tiger
through the long grass
and its spears of seeds,
and how (wrong-toothed) he eats
the long grass, or chews
and merely plays with it,
startling a safe-seeming moth —
a grey charred paper
lifting from his fire.

England, 20th century

Kobayashi Issa

Sleeping, waking,
Giving such tremendous yawns—
The cat goes courting!

Japan, 19th century
Trans. Lewis Mackenzie

Karai Senryū

Disturbed, the cat
Lifts its belly
On to its back.

Japan, 18th century
Trans. Bownas & Thwaite

Fourteen Ways of Touching the Peter

George MacBeth

I You can push
your thumb
in the
ridge
between his
shoulder-blades
to please him.

II Starting
at its root,
you can let
his whole
tail
flow
through your hand.

III Forming
a fist
you can let
him rub
his bone
skull
against it, hard.

IV When he makes
bread,
you can lift
him
by his under-
sides on your
knuckles.

V In hot
weather
you can itch
the fur
under
his chin. He
likes that.

VI At night
you can hoist
him
out of his bean-stalk,
sleepily
clutching
paper bags.

VII Pressing
his head against
your cheek,
you can carry
him
in the dark,
safely.

VIII In late Autumn
you can find
seeds
adhering
to his fur.
There are
plenty.

IX You can prise
his jaws
open,
helping
any medicine
he won't
abide, go down.

X You can touch
his
feet, only
if
he is relaxed.
He
doesn't like it.

XI You can comb
spare.thin
fur
from his coat,
so he won't
get
fur ball.

XII You can shake
his rigid
chicken-leg leg,
scouring his
hind-quarters
with his Vim
tongue.

XIII Dumping
hot fish
on his plate, you can
fend
him off,
pushing
and purring.

XIV You can have
him shrimp
along you,
breathing,
whenever
you want
to compose poems.

England, 20th century

Bimbo's Pome

Paul Klee

—In the manner of Klee's favourite cat, named Bimbo—
The Master noes what he wonts.
he noes whow.

But has one vice: not smokeing.
But skratches with wip of hoarsehair on the vielin,
that herts Bimbo so mutch in his ear.

Switzerland, 20th century
Trans. Anselm Hollo

The Panther

R. M. Rilke

His gaze, going past those bars, has got so misted
with tiredness, it can take in nothing more.
He feels as though a thousand bars existed,
and no more world beyond them than before.

Those supple powerful paddings, turning there
in tiniest of circles, well might be
the dance of forces round a centre where
some mighty will stands paralyticly.

Just now and then the pupils' noiseless shutter
is lifted.—Then an image will indart,
down through the limbs' intensive stillness flutter,
and end its being in the heart.

Germany, 20th century
Trans. J. B. Leishman

from Lady Feeding the Cats

Douglas Stewart

Shuffling along in her broken shoes from the slums,
A blue-eyed lady showing the weather's stain,
Her long dress green and black like a pine in the rain,
Her bonnet much bedraggled, daily she comes
Uphill past the Moreton Bays and the smoky gums
With a sack of bones on her back and a song in her brain
To feed those outlaws prowling about the Domain,
Those furtive she-cats and those villainous toms.

Proudly they step to meet her, they march together
With an arching of backs and a waving of plumy tails
And smiles that swear they never would harm a feather.
They rub at her legs for the bounty that never fails,
　　They think she is a princess out of a tower,
　　And so she is, she is trembling with love and power.

Australia, 20th century

61

My Parents

Stephen Spender

My parents kept me from children who were rough
Who threw words like stones and who wore torn clothes.
Their thighs showed through rags. They ran in the street
And climbed cliffs and stripped by the country streams.

I feared more than tigers their muscles like iron
Their jerking hands and their knees tight on my arms.
I feared the salt coarse pointing of those boys
Who copied my lisp behind me on the road.

They were lithe, they sprang out behind hedges
Like dogs to bark at my world. They threw mud
While I looked the other way, pretending to smile.
I longed to forgive them, but they never smiled.

England, 20th century

Silence

Marianne Moore

My father used to say,
'Superior people never make long visits,
have to be shown Longfellow's grave
or the glass flowers at Harvard.
Self-reliant like the cat—
that takes its prey to privacy,
the mouse's limp tail hanging like a shoelace from
    its mouth—
they sometimes enjoy solitude,
and can be robbed of speech
by speech which has delighted them.
The deepest feeling always shows itself in silence;
not in silence, but restraint.'
Nor was he insincere in saying, 'Make my house
    your inn.'
Inns are not residences.

U.S.A., 20th century

To My Mother

George Barker

Most near, most dear, most loved and most far,
Under the window where I often found her
Sitting as huge as Asia, seismic with laughter,
Gin and chicken helpless in her Irish hand,
Irresistible as Rabelais, but most tender for
The lame dogs and hurt birds that surround her,—
She is a procession no one can follow after
But be like a little dog following a brass band.

She will not glance up at the bomber, or condescend
To drop her gin and scuttle to a cellar,
But lean on the mahogany table like a mountain
Whom only faith can move, and so I send
O all my faith and all my love to tell her
That she will move from mourning into morning.

England, 20th century

Our Father

Ray Mathew

She said my father had whiskers and looked like God;
that he swore like a fettler, drank like a bottle;
used to run away from mother, left money for food;
called us by numbers; had a belt with a buckle.

On Sunday was churchday. We children walked behind.
He'd wear a stiff collar. He'd say good-morning.
And we made jokes about him, we were afraid
because already we understood about hating.

When we'd left the church that was so nice and still,
the minister would let us give the bells a telling—
for dong-dells; and we'd decide that Nell's
was to be the end of the world; it was time for going.

When we got home he'd take off his collar, and his shoes;
and his Sunday-special braces; and we'd whisper,
he's not like God. So that he'd belt us for the noise,
and we'd yell. And on Mondays he'd run away from mother.

Australia, 20th century

My Papa's Waltz

Theodore Roethke

The whiskey on your breath
Could make a small boy dizzy;
But I hung on like death:
Such waltzing was not easy.

We romped until the pans
Slid from the kitchen shelf;
My mother's countenance
Could not unfrown itself.

The hand that held my wrist
Was battered on one knuckle;
At every step you missed
My right ear scraped a buckle.

You beat time on my head
With a palm caked hard by dirt,
Then waltzed me off to bed
Still clinging to your shirt.

U.S.A., 20th century

To Mistress Isabel Pennell

John Skelton

By Saint Mary, my lady,
Your mammy and your daddy,
Brought forth a goodly baby!

My maiden Isabel,
Reflaring rosabel,
The fragrant camomel;
  The ruddy rosary,
The sovereign rosemary,
The pretty strawberry;
  The columbine, the nept,
The gillyflower well set,
The proper violet;
  Ennewèd your colour
Is like the daisy flower
After the April shower;
  Star of the morrow gray.
The blossom on the spray,
The freshest flower of May;
  Maidenly demure,
Of womanhood the lure;
Wherefore I make sure
  It were an heavenly health,
It were an endless wealth,
A life for God himself,
  To hear this nightingale
Among the birdës small
Warbling in the vale,
  Dug dug
Jug, jug,
  Good year and good luck
  With chuck, chuck, chuck, chuck.

England, 15th century

65

Two Spanish Gypsy Lullabies

Anon.

An angel of cinnamon
guards your cradle,
the head at the sun
the feet at the moon.

Under the laurels,
my daughter's cradle,
and when the moon rises
it calls her,
it calls her.

Spain, trad.
Trans. anon.

Child

Sylvia Plath

Your clear eye is the one absolutely beautiful thing.
I want to fill it with colours and ducks,
The zoo of the new

Whose names you meditate—
April snowdrop, Indian pipe,
Little

Stalk without a wrinkle,
Pool in which images
Should be grand and classical

Not this troublous
Wringing of hands, this dark
Ceiling without a star.

U.S.A., 20th century

66

Baby's World
Rabindranath Tagore

I wish I could take a quiet corner in the heart of my
baby's very own world.

I know it has stars that talk to him, and a sky that
stoops down to his face to amuse him with its silly
clouds and rainbows.

Those who make believe to be dumb, and look as if
they never could move, come creeping to his window
with their stories and with trays crowded with
bright toys.

I wish I could travel by the road that crosses baby's
mind, and out beyond all bounds;

Where messengers run errands for no cause between
the kingdoms of kings of no history;

Where Reason makes kites of her laws and flies
them, and Truth sets Fact free from its fetters.

India, 20th century

Karai Senryū

Now the man has a child
He knows all the names
Of the local dogs.

Japan, 18th century
Trans. Bownas & Thwaite

Childhood
Anon.

When legs beneath kilts grow sturdy and strong,
    The grass soft a-foot dew-brimming,
While skurrying dogs run barking along,
    Stones on the water go skimming.

67

When bird-songs and hens fill the barnyard air,
  And from byre there comes the lowing,
When mist on the hills is rising fair,
  All the little feet are going.

The game of 'tig' and the bare pony-ride,
  The boat on the water gleaming,
The peat fire of evening and tale beside
  Fill daytime till bedtime dreaming.

O God bless the girl and God bless the boy,
  No ragwort-whip may they merit,
And as they grow be they filled with thy joy,
  Thy kingdom may they inherit.

Scotland, trad.
Trans. G. R. D. McLean

Japanese Children

James Kirkup

The round, calm faces rosy with the cold
Are squared by a window of black hair
From which the delicate features peep:
Eyes dark sloes that slide in sleepy lids,
The happy nose, lips plump as robins.

Grave, cosy dolls in their padded clothes,
Patiently they stand in the swimming snow
Beside mother and father, quiet and good.
On the mother's back, wrapped warm inside
    her flowered cape,
The fat, drowsy baby blinks, and does not cry.

England, 20th century

Navajo Children, Canyon de Chelly, Arizona

Christopher Middleton

You sprouted from sand,
running, stopping, running;
beyond you tall red
tons of rock rested
on the feathery tamarisk.

Torn jeans, T-shirts
lope and skip, toes drum
and you're coming
full tilt
for the lollipops,

hopefully
arrive, daren't
look, for our stares
(your noses dribble)
prove too rude

in your silence,
can't break, either,
your upturned
monkey faces into smiles.
It's no joke

as you grope
up, up
to the driver's door, take
them reverently, the
lollipops—

your smallest, too small,
waited three
paces back, shuffling,
then provided,
evidently

by a sister on tiptoe who
takes his hand, helps
unwrap the sugar totem.
And we are swept
on, bouncing,

look back,
seeing walls
dwarf you. But how
could you get any
more thin, small, far.

England, 20th century

For a Junior School Poetry Book
Christopher Middleton

The mothers are waiting in the yard.
Here come the children, fresh from school.
The mothers are wearing rumpled skirts.
What prim mouths, what wrinkly cheeks.
The children swirl through the air to them,
trailing satchels and a smell of chalk.

The children are waiting in the yard.
The mothers come stumbling out of school.
The children stare primly at them,
lace their shoes, pat their heads.
The mothers swirl through the air to cars.
The children crossly drive them home.

The mothers are coming.
The children are waiting.
The mothers had eyes that see
boiled eggs, wool, dung, and bed.
The children have eyes that saw
owl and mountain and little mole.

England, 20th century

At the Railway Station, Upway

or

(The Convict and Boy with the Violin)

Thomas Hardy

'There is not much that I can do,
　For I've no money that's quite my own!'
　Spoke up the pitying child—
A little boy with a violin
At the station before the train came in,—
'But I can play my fiddle to you,
And a nice one 'tis, and good in tone!'

　The man in the handcuffs smiled;
The constable looked and he smiled too,
　As the fiddle began to twang;
And the man in the handcuffs suddenly sang
　With grimful glee:
　'This life so free
　Is the thing for me!'
And the constable smiled, and said no word,
As if unconscious of what he heard;
And so they went on till the train came in—
The convict, and boy with the violin.

England, 19th century

A Boy's Head

Miroslav Holub

In it there is a space-ship
and a project
for doing away with piano lessons.

And there is
Noah's ark,
which shall be first.

71

And there is
an entirely new bird,
an entirely new hare,
an entirely new bumble-bee.

There is a river
that flows upwards.

There is a multiplication table.

There is anti-matter.

And it just cannot be trimmed.

I believe
that only what cannot be trimmed
is a head.

There is much promise
in the circumstance
that so many people have heads.

Czechoslovakia, 20th century
Trans. Ian Milner

The Dunce

Jacques Prévert

He says no with his head
but his heart says yes
he says yes to what he likes
he says no to the teacher
he is on his feet
to be questioned
to be asked all the problems
suddenly he shakes with uncontrollable mirth

and he rubs them all out
the figures and the words
the dates and the names
the sentences and the traps
and despite the threats from the master
amid the jeers of the child prodigies
with all the coloured chalks
upon the miserable black board
he draws the face of happiness.

France, 20th century
Trans. John Dixon Hunt

Little girl, be careful what you say

Carl Sandburg

Little girl, be careful what you say
when you make talk with words, words—
for words are made of syllables
and syllables, child, are made of air—
and air is so thin—air is the breath of God—
air is finer than fire or mist,
finer than water or moonlight,
finer than spiderwebs in the moon,
finer than water-flowers in the morning:
   and words are strong, too,
   stronger than rocks or steel
stronger than potatoes, corn, fish, cattle,
and soft, too, soft as little pigeon-eggs,
soft as the music of humming bird wings.
   So, little girl, when you speak greetings,
when you tell jokes, make wishes or prayers,
   be careful, be careless, be careful.
   be what you wish to be.

U.S.A., 20th century

Child Margaret

Carl Sandburg

The child Margaret begins to write numbers on a Saturday
    morning, the first numbers formed under her wishing child
    fingers.
All the numbers come well-born, shaped in figures assertive for a
    frieze in a child's room.
Both 1 and 7 are straightforward, military, filled with lunge and
    attack, erect in shoulder-straps.
The 6 and 9 salute as dancing sisters, elder and younger, and 2 is a
    trapeze actor swinging to handclaps.
All the numbers are well-born, only 3 has a hump on its back and
    8 is knock-kneed.
The child Margaret kisses all once and gives two kisses to 3 and 8.
(Each number is a brand-new rag doll . . . O in the wishing
    fingers . . . millions of rag dolls, millions and millions of new
    rag dolls!!)

U.S.A., 20th century

The Collegiate Angels

Rafael Alberti

None of us understood the secret dark of the blackboards
nor why the armillary sphere seemed so remote when we
    looked at it.
We only knew that a circumference does not have to be round
and that an eclipse of the moon confuses the flowers
and speeds up the timing of birds.

None of us understood anything:
nor why our fingers were made of India ink
and the afternoon closed compasses only to have the dawn
    open books.
We only knew that a straight line, if it likes, can be curved
    or broken
and that the wandering stars are children who don't know
    arithmetic.

Spain, 20th century
Trans. Mark Strand

A Snowy Day in School

D. H. Lawrence

All the long school-hours, round the irregular hum
    of the class
Have pressed immeasurable spaces of hoarse silence
Muffling my mind, as snow muffles the sounds that
    pass
Down the soiled street. We have pattered the
    lessons ceaselessly—

But the faces of the boys, in the brooding, yellow light
Have been for me like a dazed constellation of stars,
Like half-blown flowers dimly shaking at the night,
Like half-seen froth on an ebbing shore in the moon.

Out of each face, strange, dark beams that disquiet;
In the open depths of each flower, dark, restless
    drops;
Twin-bubbling challenge and mystery, in the foam's
    whispering riot.
—How can I answer the challenge of so many eyes?

The thick snow is crumpled on the roof, it plunges
    down
Awfully!—Must I call back a hundred eyes?—A voice

Falters a statement about an abstract noun—
What was my question?—My God, must I break
    this hoarse

Silence that rustles beyond the stars?—There!—
I have startled a hundred eyes, and now I must look
Them an answer back; it is more than I can bear.

The snow descends as if the slow sky shook
In flakes of shadow down; while through the gap
Between the schools sweeps one black rook.

In the playground, a shaggy snowball stands huge
    and still
With fair flakes lighting down on it. Beyond, the
    town
Is lost in this shadowed silence the skies distil.

And all things are in silence, they can brood
Alone within the dim and hoarse silence.
Only I and the class must wrangle; this work is a
    bitter rood!

England, 20th century

The Herdboy

Lu Yu

In the southern village the boy who minds the ox
With his naked feet stands on the ox's back.
Through the hole in his coat the river wind blows;
Through his broken hat the mountain rain pours.
On the long dyke he seemed to be far away;
In the narrow lane suddenly we were face to face.

The boy is home and the ox is back in its stall;
And a dark smoke oozes through the thatched roof.

China, 12th century
Trans. Arthur Waley

Farm Child

R. S. Thomas

Look at this village boy, his head is stuffed
With all the nests he knows, his pockets with flowers,
Snail-shells and bits of glass, the fruit of hours
Spent in the fields by thorn and thistle tuft.
Look at his eyes, see the harebell hiding there;
Mark how the sun has freckled his smooth face
Like a finch's egg under that bush of hair
That dares the wind, and in the mixen now
Notice his poise; from such unconscious grace
Earth breeds and beckons to the stubborn plough.

Wales, 20th century

Abraham and Isaac

(from the Chester Miracle Play)

Anon.

GOD: Abraham, my servant, Abraham.

ABRAHAM: Lo, Lord, all ready here I am.

GOD:

Take, Isaac, thy son by name,
That thou lovest the best of all,
And in sacrifice offer him to me
Upon that hill there beside thee.
Abraham, I will that so it be,
For ought that may befall.

ABRAHAM:

My Lord, to thee is mine intent
Ever to be obedient.
That son that thou to me hath sent,
Offer I will to thee . . .
Thy bidding done shall be . . .

(*Here* ABRAHAM, *turning him to his son Isaac, saith:*)
Make thee ready, my dear darling,
For we must do a little thing.
This wood do on thy back it bring,
We may no longer abide.
A sword and fire that I will take;   (*Here Abraham taketh*
For sacrifice me behoves to make: *a sword and fire.*)
God's bidding will I not forsake,
But ever obedient be.

(*Here* ISAAC *speaketh to his father, and taketh a bundle of sticks and beareth after his father, and saith:*)
Father, I am all ready
To do your bidding most meekly,
And to bear this wood full beane am I,
As you commanded me . . .

(*Here they go both to the place to do sacrifice*)

78

ABRAHAM:

Now, Isaac son, go we our way
To yonder mount, if that we may.

ISAAC:

My dear father, I will assay
To follow you full fain.

(ABRAHAM, *being minded to slay his son Isaac, lifts up his hands, and
saith the following:*)

Ho! my heart will break in three,
To hear thy words I have pity;
As thou wilt, Lord, so must it be,
To thee I will be bayne.
Lay down thy faggot, my own son dear.

ISAAC:

All ready, father, lo it is here.
But why make you such heavy cheer?
Are you any thing adread?
Father, if it be your will,
Where is the beast that we shall kill?

ABRAHAM:

Thereof, son, is none upon this hill,
That I see here in stead.

(ISAAC, *fearing lest his father would slay him, saith:*)

Father, I am full sore afraid
To see you bear that drawn sword:
I hope for all middle earde
You will not slay your child.

(ABRAHAM *comforts his son, and saith:*)

Dread thee not, my child, I read;
Our Lord will send of his godhead
Some manner of beast into this field,
Either tame or wild.

ISAAC:

Father, tell me or I go
Whether I shall be harmed or no.

ABRAHAM:

    Ah! dear God! that me is woe!
    Thou breaks my heart asunder . . .
    Isaac, son, peace, I thee pray,
    Thou breaks my heart in twaie.

ISAAC:

    I pray you, father, hide nothing from me,
    But tell me what you think.

ABRAHAM:

    Ah! Isaac, Isaac, I must thee kill!

ISAAC:

    Alas! father, is that your will,
    Your own child for to spill
    Upon this hill's brink?
    If I have trespassed in any degree,
    With a yard you may beat me;
    Put up your sword, if your will be,
    For I am but a child.

ABRAHAM:

    O, my dear son, I am sorry
    To do to thee this great annoy.
    God's commandment do must I,
    His works are ever full mild.

ISAAC:

    Would God my mother were here with me!
    She would kneel down upon her knee,
    Praying you, father, if it may be,
    For to save my life . . .
    Is it God's will I shall be slain?

ABRAHAM:

    Yea, son, it is not for to lean;
    To his bidding I will be bayn,
    And ever to him pleasing.
    But that I do this doleful deed,
    My Lord will not quit me in my need . . .

(*Here* ISAAC *asking his father's blessing on his knees, and saith:*)
Father, seeing you must needs do so,
Let it pass lightly, and over go;
Kneeling on my knees two,
Your blessing on me spread. . . .
Father, I pray you hide my eyes,
That I see not the sword so keen;
Your stroke, father, would I not see,
Lest I against it cry.

ABRAHAM:
My dear son Isaac speak no more,
Thy words make my heart full sore.

ISAAC:
O dear father, wherefore! wherefore!
Seeing I must needs be dead,
Of one thing I will you pray,
Seeing I must die the death today,
As few strokes you will make,
When you smite off my head.

ABRAHAM:
Thy meekness, child, makes me afraid;
My song may be wail-a-way.

ISAAC:
O dear father, do away, do away
Your making so much moan!
Now, truly, father, this talking
Doth but make long tarrying,
I pray you, come and make ending,
And let me hence be gone.

(*Here Isaac riseth and cometh to his father, and he taketh him and
bindeth and layeth him upon the altar to sacrifice him, and saith:*)
ABRAHAM:
Come hither, my child, thou art so sweet,
Thou must be bound both hand and feet.

ISAAC:
Father, we must no more meet,

Be ought that I may see;
But do with me then as you will,
I must obey, and that is skill,
God's commandment to fulfil,
For needs so must it be . . .
Father, greet well my brethren young,
And pray my mother of her blessing,
I come no more under her wing,
Fare well for ever and aye;
But, father, I cry you mercy,
For all that ever I have trespassed to thee,
Forgiven, father, that it may be
Until domesday.

ABRAHAM:
My dear son, let be thy moans!
My child, thou grieved me never once;
Blessed be thou body and bones,
And I forgive thee here!
Now, my dear son, here shalt thou lie,
Unto my work now must I hie;
I had as well my self to die,
As thou, my dear darling.

ISAAC:
Father, if you be to me kind,
About my head a kerchief bind,
And let me lightly out of your mind,
And soon that I were sped.

(*Here Abraham doth kiss his son Isaac, and binds a kerchief about his head.*)

ABRAHAM: Fare well, my sweet son of grace!

(*Here let* ISAAC *kneel down and speak*:)
I pray you, father, turn down my face
A little, while you have space,
For I am full sore adread.

ABRAHAM: To do this deed I am sorry.

ISAAC:
Yea, Lord, to thee I call and cry,

Of my soul thou have mercy,
Heartily I thee pray!

ABRAHAM:

Lord, I would fain work thy will,
This young innocent that lieth so still
Full loth were me him to kill,
By any manner a way . . .

ISAAC:

Ah! mercy, father, why tarry you so?
Smite off my head and let me go.
I pray rid me of my woe,
For now I take my leave.

ABRAHAM:

Ah! son! my heart will break in three,
To hear thee speak such words to me.
Jesu! on me thou have pity
That I have most in mind.

ISAAC:

Now, father I see that I shall die:
Almighty God in majesty!
My soul I offer unto thee;
Lord, to it be kind.

(*Here let Abraham take and bind his son Isaac upon the altar; let him make a sign as though he would cut off his head with his sword; then let the angel come and take the sword by the end and stay it, saying:*)

ANGELLUS: Abraham, my servant dear.

ABRAHAM: Lo, Lord, I am all ready here!

ANGELLUS:

Lay not thy sword in no manner
On Isaac, thy dear darling;
And do to him no annoy.
For thou dreads God, well wot I,
That of thy son has no mercy,
To fulfil his bidding.

83

SECUNDUS ANGELLUS:

    And for his bidding thou dost aye,
    And sparest neither for fear nor fray,
    To do thy son to death to day,
    Isaac, to thee full dear:
    Therefore, God hath sent by me, in fay
    A lamb, that is both good and gay,
    To have him right here.

ABRAHAM:

    Ah! Lord of heaven, and king of bliss,
    Thy bidding shall be done, i-wiss!
    Sacrifice here sent me is,
    And all, Lord, through thy grace.
    A horned wether here I see,
    Among the briars tied is he,
    To thee offered shall he be,
    Anon right in this place.

(*Then let Abraham take the lamb and kill him, and let* GOD *say:*)

    Abraham, by my self I swear,
    For thou hast been obedient ever,
    And spared not thy son to tear,
    To fulfil my bidding,
    Thou shall be blessed, that pleasèd me,
    Thy seed I shall so multiply,
    As stars and sand so many heigh I,
    Of thy body coming.
    Of enemies thou shalt have power,
    And of thy blood also in fear,
    Thou hast been meek and bonere,
    And do as I thee bade;
    And of all nations, leve thou me,
    Blessed ever more shall thou be,
    Through fruit that shall come of thee,
    And saved be through thy seed.

England, medieval

The Hermit

Hsü Pên

I dwell apart
From the world of men.

I lift my eyes
To the mighty hills,
And sit in silent reverie
By rushing streams.
My songs
Are the whisperings of the winds
And the soft murmurs
Of falling rain.

Blossoms open
And flutter to earth again.
Men come
And men go;
Year follows year,
And life goes on.

China, 18th century
Trans. Henry H. Hart

Ode on Solitude

Alexander Pope

Happy the man whose wish and care
  A few paternal acres bound,
Content to breath his native air,
    In his own ground.

Whose herds with milk, whose fields with bread,
  Whose flocks supply him with attire,
Whose trees in summer yield him shade,
    In winter fire.

Blessed, who can unconcern'dly find
    Hours, days, and years slide soft away,
In health of body, peace of mind,
        Quiet by day,

Sound sleep by night; study and ease,
    Together mixed; sweet recreation;
And innocence which most does please
        With meditation.

Thus let me live, unseen, unknown,
    Thus unlamented let me die,
Steal from the world, and not a stone
        Tell where I lie.

England, 18th century

The Three Hermits

W. B. Yeats

Three old hermits took the air
By a cold and desolate sea,
First was muttering a prayer,
Second rummaged for a flea;
On a windy stone, the third,
Giddy with his hundredth year,
Sang unnoticed like a bird:
'Though the Door of Death is near
And what waits behind the door,
Three times in a single day
I, though upright on the shore,
Fall asleep when I should pray.'
So the first, but now the second:
'We're but given what we have earned
When all thoughts and deeds are reckoned,

86

So it's plain to be discerned
That the shades of holy men
Who have failed, being weak of will,
Pass the Door of Birth again,
And are plagued by crowds, until
They've the passion to escape.'
Moaned the other, 'They are thrown
Into some most fearful shape.'
But the second mocked his moan:
'They are not changed to anything,
Having loved God once, but maybe
To a poet or a king
Or a witty lovely lady.'
While he'd rummaged rags and hair,
Caught and cracked his flea, the third,
Giddy with his hundredth year,
Sang unnoticed like a bird.

Ireland, 20th century

Casual Lines

Su Shih

A lonely, sickly old man,
I make my home
On the Eastern Embankment.

My beard, bleached by the frost
And combed by the wind,
Is becoming more and more sparse.

This morning my little boy
Was pleasantly surprised
To find roses grow once more on my cheeks.

I smiled,
For he did not know
I had just taken a little wine.

China, 11th century
Trans. Teresa Li

The Eastern Gate

Anon.

I went out at the eastern gate;
I never thought to return.
But I came back to the gate with my heart full of sorrow.
There was not a peck of rice in the bin;
There was not a coat hanging on the pegs.
So I took my sword and went towards the gate.
My wife and child clutched at my coat and wept;
'Some people want to be rich and grand;
I only want to share my porridge with you.
Above, we have the blue waves of the sky;
Below, the face of this child that suckles at my breast.'
    'Dear wife, I cannot stay.
    Soon it will be too late.
    When one is growing old
    One cannot put things off.'

China, 1st century
Trans. Arthur Waley

And the days are not full enough

Ezra Pound

And the days are not full enough
And the nights are not full enough
And life slips by like a field-mouse.
      Not shaking the grass.

U.S.A., 20th century

The Little Cart

Ch'ên Tzû-lung

The little cart jolting and banging through the yellow haze
    of dusk;
The man pushing behind, the woman pulling in front.
They have left the city and do not know where to go.
'Green, green, those elm-tree leaves: *they* will cure my hunger,
If only we could find some quiet place and sup on them together.'

  The wind has flattened the yellow mother-wort;
  Above it in the distance they see the walls of a house.
'*There* surely must be people living who'll give you something to
    eat.'
They tap at the door, but no one comes; they look in, but the
    kitchen is empty.
They stand hesitating in the lonely road and their tears fall like
    rain.

China, 17th century
Trans. Arthur Waley

Saint Francis and the Birds

Seamus Heaney

When Francis preached love to the birds
They listened, fluttered, throttled up
Into the blue like a flock of words

Released for fun from his holy lips.
Then wheeled back, whirred about his head,
Pirouetted on brothers' capes,

Danced on the wing, for sheer joy played
And sang, like images took flight.
Which was the best poem Francis made,

His argument true, his tone light.

Ireland, 20th century

Proud Songsters

Thomas Hardy

The thrushes sing as the sun is going,
  And the finches whistle in ones and pairs,
And as it gets dark loud nightingales
    In bushes
Pipe, as they can when April wears,
  As if all Time were theirs.

These are brand-new birds of twelve-months'
      growing,
Which a year ago, or less than twain,
No finches were, nor nightingales,
    Nor thrushes,
But only particles of grain,
  And earth, and air, and rain.

England, 20th century

A Blackbird Singing

R. S. Thomas

It seems wrong that out of this bird,
Black, bold, a suggestion of dark
Places about it, there yet should come
Such rich music, as though the notes'
Ore were changed to a rare metal
At one touch of that bright bill.

You have heard it often, alone at your desk
In a green April, your mind drawn
Away from its work by sweet disturbance
Of the mild evening outside your room.

A slow singer, but loading each phrase
With history's overtones, love, joy
And grief learned by his dark tribe
In other orchards and passed on
Instinctively as they are now,
But fresh always with new tears.

Wales, 20th century

The Starling

John Heath-Stubbs

The starling is my darling, although
I don't much approve of its
Habits. Proletarian bird,
Nesting in holes and corners, making a mess,
And sometimes dropping its eggs
Just any old where—on the front lawn, for instance.

It thinks it can sing too. In springtime
They are on every rooftop, or high bough,
Or telegraph pole, blithering away
Discords, with clichés picked up
From the other melodists.

But go to Trafalgar Square,
And stand, about sundown, on the steps of St Martin's;
Mark then, in the air,
The starlings, before they roost, at their evolutions—
Scores of starlings, wheeling,
Streaming and twisting, the whole murmuration
Turning like one bird: an image
Realised, of the City.

England, 20th century

The Hawk

W. B. Yeats

'Call down the hawk from the air;
Let him be hooded or caged
Till the yellow eye has grown mild,
For larder and spit are bare,
The old cook enraged,
The scullion gone wild.'

'I will not be clapped in a hood,
Nor a cage, nor alight upon wrist,
Now I have learnt to be proud
Hovering over the wood
In the broken mist
Or tumbling cloud.'

'What tumbling cloud did you cleave,
Yellow-eyed hawk of the mind,
Last evening? that I, who had sat
Dumbfounded before a knave,
Should give to my friend
A pretence of wit.'

Ireland, 20th century

Perfect

Glyn Jones

I found a pigeon's skull on the machair,
All the bones pure white and dry, and chalky,
But perfect,
Without a crack or a flaw anywhere.

At the back, rising out of the beak,
Were domes like bubbles of thin bone,
Almost transparent, where the brain had been
That fixed the tilt of the wings.

Wales, 20th century
(See note on p. 300)

Karai Senryū

The chicken wants
To say something—
Fidgeting its feet.

Japan, 18th century
Trans. Bownas & Thwaite

Naitō Jōsō

'I've seen everything,
Right to the bottom of the pond'—
The look on the duckling's face.

Japan, 17th century
Trans. Bownas & Thwaite,
ed. D.M.

Karai Senryū

With his apology
For wings, as best he can
The duck flies.

Japan, 18th century
Trans. Bownas & Thwaite

Poor Bird

Walter de la Mare

Poor bird!—
No hands, no fingers thine;
Two angel-coloured wings instead:
But where are mine?

Cold voiceless fish!—
No hands, no spindly legs, no toes;
But fins and a tail,
And a mouth for nose.

93

Wild weed!—
Not even an eye with which to see!
Or ear, or tongue,
For sigh or song;
Or heart to beat,
Or mind to long.

And yet—ah, would that I,
In sun and shade, like thee,
Might no less gentle, sweet,
And lovely be!

England, 20th century

Cormorants
John Blight

The sea has it this way: if you see
Cormorants, they are the pattern for the eye.
In the sky, on the rocks, in the water, shags!
To think of them every way: I see them, oily rags
Flung starboard from some tramp and washed
On to rocks, flung up by the waves, squashed
Into sock-shapes with the foot up; sooty birds
Wearing white, but not foam-white; swearing not words,
But blaspheming with swastika-gesture, wing-hinge to nose;
Ugly grotesqueries, all in a shag's pose.
And beautifully ugly for their being shags,
Not partly swans. When the eye searches for rags,
It does not seek muslin, white satin; nor,
For its purpose, does the sea adorn shags more.

Australia, 20th century

And Other Poems

R. S. Morgan

The swan switches its tail and plugs
Its beak into the river bed;
Or the lumpy pillow follows its
White upright rolled umbrella head,

While webbed feet fall from the sycamore tree,
And, at our gardening steps, the sparrows,
Guerrilla-like, lurk under the hollies,
And the starlings squeal like wheelbarrows.

The brashest elephants shy at screeds
But like, like dogs, a quick run in the park.
There are no butterflies on me,
I keep things short and dark.

England, 20th century

My Sister Jane

Ted Hughes

And I say nothing—no, not a word
About our Jane. Haven't you heard?
She's a bird, a bird, a bird, a bird.
Oh it never would do to let folks know
My sister's nothing but a great big crow.

Each day (we daren't send her to school)
She pulls on stockings of thick blue wool
To make her pin crow legs look right,
Then fits a wig of curls on tight,
And dark spectacles—a huge pair
To cover her very crowy stare.
Oh it never would do to let folks know
My sister's nothing but a great big crow.

95

When visitors come she sits upright
(With her wings and her tail tucked out of sight).
They think her queer but extremely polite.
Then when the visitors have gone
She whips out her wings and with her wig on
Whirls through the house at the height of your head—
Duck, duck, or she'll knock you dead.
Oh it never would do to let folks know
My sister's nothing but a great big crow.

At meals whatever she sees she'll stab it—
Because she's a crow and that's a crow habit.
My mother says 'Jane! Your manners! Please!'
Then she'll sit quietly on the cheese,
Or play the piano nicely by dancing on the keys—
Oh it never would do to let folks know
My sister's nothing but a great big crow.

England, 20th century

To Paint the Portrait of a Bird

Jacques Prévert

First paint a cage
with an open door
then paint
something pretty
something simple
something beautiful
something useful . . .
for the bird
then place the canvas against a tree
in a garden
in a wood
or in a forest
hide behind the tree
without speaking

without moving . . .
Sometimes the bird comes quickly
but he can just as well spend long years
before deciding
Don't get discouraged
wait
wait years if necessary
the swiftness or slowness of the coming
of the bird having no rapport
with the success of the picture
When the bird comes
if he comes
observe the most profound silence
wait till the bird enters the cage
and when he has entered
gently close the door with a brush
then
paint out all the bars one by one
taking care not to touch any of the feathers of the bird
Then paint the portrait of the tree
choosing the most beautiful of its branches
for the bird
paint also the green foliage and the wind's freshness
the dust of the sun
and the noise of insects in the summer heat
and then wait for the bird to begin to sing
If the bird doesn't sing
it's a bad sign
a sign that the painting is bad
but if he sings it's a good sign
a sign that you can sign
So then so very gently you pull out
one of the feathers of the bird
and you write your name in a corner of the picture.

France, 20th century
Trans. Lawrence Ferlinghetti

97

Turkeys Observed

Seamus Heaney

One observes them, one expects them;
Blue-breasted in their indifferent mortuary,
Bleached bare on the cold marble slabs
In immodest underwear frills of feather.

The red sides of beef retain
Some of the smelly majesty of living:
A half-cow slung from a hook maintains
That blood and flesh are not ignored.

But a turkey cowers in death.
Pull his neck, pluck him, and look—
He is just another poor forked thing,
A skin bag plumped with inky putty.

He once complained extravagantly
In an overture of gobbles;
He lorded it on the claw-flecked mud
With a grey flick of his Confucian eye.

Now, as I pass the bleak Christmas dazzle,
I find him ranged with his cold squadrons:
The fuselage is bare, the proud wings snapped,
The tail-fan stripped down to a shameful rudder.

Ireland, 20th century

Roast Swan Song

Anon.

Aforetime, by the waters wan,
This lovely body I put on:
In life I was a stately swan.

Ah me! Ah me!
Now browned and basted thoroughly.

The cook now turns me round and turns me.
The hurrying waiter next concerns me,
But oh, this fire, how fierce it burns me!

Ah me! Ah me!

Would I might glide, my plumage fluffing,
On pools to feel the cool wind soughing,
Rather than burst with pepper-stuffing.

Ah me! Ah me!

Once I was whiter than the snow,
The fairest bird that earth could show;
Now I am blacker than the crow.

Ah me! Ah me!

Here I am dished upon the platter.
I cannot fly. Oh, what's the matter?
Lights flash, teeth clash—I fear the latter.

Ouch! . . . Ouch! . . .

Bavaria, 13th century
Trans. from the Latin by
George F. Whicher

South Wind

Tu Fu

The days grow long, the mountains
Beautiful. The south wind blows
Over blossoming meadows.
Newly arrived swallows dart
Over the steaming marshes.
Ducks in pairs drowse on the warm sand.

China, 8th century
Trans. Kenneth Rexroth

from Phrases

Jean-Nicolas-Arthur Rimbaud

I have stretched ropes from belfry to belfry;
garlands from window to window;
golden chains from star to star,
and I am dancing.

France, 19th century
Trans. Oliver Bernard

Miracles

Walt Whitman

Why, who makes much of a miracle?
As to me I know of nothing else but miracles,
Whether I walk the streets of Manhattan,
Or dart my sight over the roofs of houses toward the sky,
Or wade with naked feet along the beach just in the edge of the
    water,
Or stand under trees in the woods,
Or talk by day with anyone I love, or sleep in the bed at night
    with anyone I love,

Or sit at table at dinner with the rest,
Or look at strangers opposite me riding in the car,
Or watch honey-bees busy around the hive of a summer fore-noon,
Or animals feeding in the fields,
Or birds, or the wonderfulness of insects in the air,
Or the wonderfulness of the sundown, or the stars shining so quiet
    and bright,
Or the exquisite delicate thin curve of the new moon in spring;
These with the rest, one and all, are to me miracles,
The whole referring, yet each distinct and in its place.

To me every hour of the light and dark is a miracle,
Every cubic inch of space is a miracle,
Every square yard of the surface of the earth is spread with the
    same,
Every foot of the interior swarms with the same.

To me the sea is a continual miracle,
The fishes that swim—the rocks—the motion of the waves—the
    ships with men in them,
What stranger miracles are there?

U.S.A., 19th century

Pied Beauty

Gerard Manley Hopkins

Glory be to God for dappled things—
    For skies of couple-colour as a brinded cow;
        For rose-moles all in stipple upon trout that swim;
Fresh-firecoal chestnut-falls; finches' wings;
    Landscape plotted and pieced—fold, fallow, and plough;
        And áll trádes, their gear and tackle and trim.

All things counter, original, spare, strange;
    Whatever is fickle, freckled (who knows how?)
        With swift, slow; sweet, sour; adazzle, dim;
He fathers-forth whose beauty is past change:
        Praise him.

England, 19th century

Matsuo Bashō

Nothing in the voice of the cicada
Intimates
How soon it will die.

Japan, 17th century
Trans. R. H. Blyth

Watanabe Suiha

The noisy cricket
Soaks up the moonbeams
On the wet lawn.

Japan, 20th century
Trans. Bownas & Thwaite

The Cicadas

Judith Wright

On yellow days in summer when the early heat
presses like hands hardening the sown earth
into stillness, when after sunrise birds fall quiet
and streams sink in their beds and in silence meet,
then underground the blind nymphs waken and move.
They must begin at last to struggle towards love.

For a whole life they have crouched alone and dumb
in patient ugliness enduring the humble dark.
Nothing has shaken that world below the world
except the far-off thunder, the strain of roots in storm.
Sunk in an airless night they neither slept nor woke
but hanging on the tree's blood dreamed vaguely the dreams
    of the tree,
and put on wavering leaves, wing-veined, too delicate to see.

But now in terror overhead their day of dying breaks.
The trumpet of the rising sun bursts into sound
and the implacable unborn stir and reply.
In the hard shell an unmade body wakes
and fights to break from its motherly-enclosing ground.
These dead must dig their upward grave in fear
to cast the living into the naked air.

Terrible is the pressure of light into the heart.
The womb is withered and cracked, the birth is begun,
and shuddering and groaning to break that iron grasp
the new is delivered as the old is torn apart.
Love whose unmerciful blade has pierced us through,
we struggle naked from our death in search of you.

This is the wild light that our dreams foretold
while unaware we prepared these eyes and wings—
while in our sleep we learned the song the world sings.
Sing now, my brothers; climb to that intolerable gold.

Australia, 20th century

Omen

Birago Diop

A naked sun—a yellow sun
A sun all naked at early dawn
Pours waves of gold over the bank
Of the river of yellow.

A naked sun—a white sun
A sun all naked and white
Pours waves of silver
Over the river of white.

A naked sun—a red sun
A sun all naked and red
Pours waves of red blood
Over the river of red.

Senegal, 20th century
Trans. from the French by
Moore & Beier

Binsey Poplars

felled 1879

Gerard Manley Hopkins

My aspens dear, whose airy cages quelled,
Quelled or quenched in leaves the leaping sun,
All felled, felled, are all felled;
    Of a fresh and following folded rank
        Not spared, not one
           That dandled a sandalled
        Shadow that swam or sank
On meadow and river and wind-wandering weed-
    winding bank.

    O if we but knew what we do
        When we delve or hew—
    Hack and rack the growing green!
        Since country is so tender
    To touch, her being só slender,
    That, like this sleek and seeing ball
    But a prick will make no eye at all,
    Where we, even where we mean
        To mend her we end her,
    When we hew or delve:
After-comers cannot guess the beauty been.
    Ten or twelve, only ten or twelve
    Strokes of havoc únselve
        The sweet especial scene,
    Rural scene, a rural scene,
    Sweet especial rural scene.

England, 19th century

The Poplar Field

William Cowper

The poplars are felled; farewell to the shade
And the whispering sound of the cool colonnade;
The winds play no longer and sing in the leaves,
Nor Ouse on his bosom their image receives.

Twelve years have elapsed since I first took a view
Of my favourite field and the bank where they grew:
And now in the grass behold they are laid,
And the tree is my seat that once lent me a shade.

The blackbird has fled to another retreat,
Where the hazels afford him a screen from the heat;
And the scene where his melody charmed me before
Resounds with his sweet-flowing ditty no more.

My fugitive years are all hasting away,
And I must ere long lie as lowly as they,
With a turf on my breast and a stone at my head,
Ere another such grove shall arise in its stead.

'Tis a sight to engage me, if anything can,
To muse on the perishing pleasures of man;
Though his life be a dream, his enjoyments, I see,
Have a being less durable even than he.

England, 18th century

The Redwoods

Louis Simpson

Mountains are moving, rivers
are hurrying. But we
are still.

We have the thoughts of giants—
clouds, and at night the stars.

And we have names—guttural, grotesque—
Hamet, Og—names with no syllables.

And perish, one by one, our roots
gnawed by the mice. And fall.

And are too slow for death, and change
to stone. Or else too quick,

like candles in a fire. Giants
are lonely. We have waited long

for someone. By our waiting, surely
there must be someone at whose touch

our boughs would bend; and hands
to gather us; a spirit

to whom we are light as the hawthorn tree.
O if there is a poet

let him come now! We stand at the Pacific
like great unmarried girls,

turning in our heads the stars and clouds,
considering whom to please.

U.S.A., 20th century

from Symmetries and Asymmetries

W. H. Auden

Leaning out over
The dreadful precipice,
One contemptuous tree.

U.S.A., 20th century

Pruning Trees

Po Chü-i

Trees growing—right in front of my window;
The trees are high and the leaves grow thick.
Sad alas! the distant mountain view,
Obscured by this, dimly shows between.
One morning I took knife and axe;
With my own hand I lopped the branches off.
Ten thousand leaves fell about my head;
A thousand hills came before my eyes.
Suddenly, as when clouds or mists break
And straight through, the blue sky appears.
Again, like the face of a friend one has loved
Seen at last after an age of parting.
First there came a gentle wind blowing;
One by one the birds flew back to the tree.
To ease my mind I gazed to the South-East;
As my eyes wandered, my thoughts went far away.
Of men there is none that has not some preference;
Of things there is none but mixes good with ill.
It was not that I did not love the tender branches;
But better still—to see the green hills!

China, 9th century
Trans. Arthur Waley

107

Telephone Poles

John Updike

They have been with us a long time.
They will outlast the elms.
Our eyes, like the eyes of a savage sieving the trees
In his search for game,
Run through them. They blend along small-town streets
Like a race of giants that have faded into mere mythology.
Our eyes, washed clean of belief,
Lift incredulous to their fearsome crowns of bolts, trusses,
     struts, nuts, insulators, and such
Barnacles as compose
These weathered encrustations of electrical debris—
Each a Gorgon's head, which, seized right,
Could stun us to stone.

Yet they are ours. We made them.
See here, where the cleats of linemen
Have roughened a second bark
Onto the bald trunk. And these spikes
Have been driven sideways at intervals handy for human
     legs.
The Nature of our construction is in every way
A better fit than the Nature it displaces.
What other tree can you climb where the birds' twitter,
Unscrambled, is English? True, their thin shade is negligible,
But then again there is not that tragic autumnal
Casting-off of leaves to outface annually.
These giants are more constant than evergreens
By being never green.

U.S.A., 20th century

The Line-Gang

Robert Frost

Here come the line-gang pioneering by.
They throw a forest down less cut than broken.
They plant dead trees for living, and the dead
They string together with a living thread.
They string an instrument against the sky
Wherein words whether beaten out or spoken
Will run as hushed as when they were a thought
But in no hush they string it: they go past
With shouts afar to pull the cable taut,
To hold it hard until they make it fast,
To ease away—they have it. With a laugh,
An oath of towns that set the wild at naught
They bring the telephone and telegraph.

U.S.A , 20th century

from Symmetries and Asymmetries

W. H. Auden

Deep in earth's opaque mirror,
The old oak's roots
Reflected its branches:

Astrologers in reverse,
Keen-eyed miners
Conned their scintillant gems.

U.S.A., 20th century

The Garden of a London House

Brian Jones

The garden of a London house;
New tenants yearly—
It wasn't hard to find excuse
For looking rarely

At coarsening grass and riotous hedge
And earth trod solid,
Easier still never to budge
And work upon it.

But something in the April airs
This Sunday morning
Prevailed. I borrow fork and shears
And fell to working

Shy in my shirtsleeves. Blunted steel
Yanked grass like tweezers
And taught me the more patient skill
Of snipping pieces

Deft from the blade-tops, in a slow
Whittling down
Towards the packed root-stalks, all yellow,
Dank from no sun.

And here, in this low world, my gaze
(First time for months)
Focused; things from void took size;
I witnessed ants

Spontaneously appear on stones,
A magic spider,
A snail's intense life through its horns'
Translucent quiver.

To shape the hedge from its neglect
I used a saw,

Relished each merciless attack,
Each soft white scar,

And how the clipped leaves from the shears
Leapt and swarmed down,
And how on the grey street appeared
Unusual green.

And now, washed, tired, in starched, clean shirt,
With blistered hands,
I gaze where I have made a start
To make amends,

And taste a weariness again
That is a pleasure
And marvel as a windless rain
Unlocks such savour

As I remember once to have known,
Or perhaps never,
For I have been long in a town
And am not a gardener.

England, 20th century

The Red Wheelbarrow

William Carlos Williams

so much depends
upon

a red wheel
barrow

glazed with rain
water

beside the white
chickens

U.S.A., 20th century

The Faun

Ezra Pound

Ha! sir, I have seen you sniffing and snoozling about among my
  flowers.
And what, pray, do you know about horticulture, you capriped?
'Come, Auster, come, Apeliota,
And see the faun in our garden.
But if you move or speak
This thing will run at you
And scare itself to spasms.'

U.S.A., 20th century

Flowers

Jean-Nicolas-Arthur Rimbaud

From a golden step—
among cords of silk, grey gauzes, green velvets,
and discs of crystal
which darken like bronze in the sun—
I see the foxgloves
opening on a carpet of silver filigree,
of eyes,
and of hair.

Coins of yellow gold sown on agate,
columns of mahogany
supporting a dome of emeralds,
bunches of white satin,
and of fine sprays of rubies
surround the water-rose.

Like a god with huge blue eyes
and shapes of snow,
the sea and the sky draw to the marble terraces
the throng of young vigorous roses.

France, 19th century
Trans. Oliver Bernard

from The Georgics
Book IV, lines 1–41, 51–57
Virgil

Next I come to the manna, the heavenly gift of honey.
Look kindly on this part too, my friend. I'll tell of a tiny
Republic that makes a show well worth your admiration—
Great-hearted leaders, a whole nation whose work is planned,
Their morals, groups, defences—I'll tell you in due order.
A featherweight theme: but one that can load me with fame, if only
No wicked fairy cross me, and the Song-god come to my call.
  For a start you must find your bees a suitable home, a position
Sheltered from wind (for wind will stop them carrying home
Their forage), a close where sheep nor goats come butting in
To jump on the flowers, nor blundering heifer stray to flick
The dew from the meadow and stamp its springing grasses down.
Discourage the lizard, too, with his lapis-lazuli back,
From their rich folds, the bee-eater and other birds,
And the swallow whose breast was blooded once by a killer's hand:
For these wreak wholesale havoc, snap up your bees on the wing
And bear them off as a tit-bit for their ungentle nestlings.
But mind there's a bubbling spring nearby, a pool moss-bordered,
And a rill ghosting through the grass:
See, too, that a palm or tall oleaster shadow the entrance,
For thus, when the new queens lead out the earliest swarms—
The spring all theirs—and the young bees play, from hive
    unprisoned,
The bank may be handy to welcome them in out of the heat
And the tree meet them halfway and make them at home in its
    foliage.
Whether the water flows or is stagnant, fling in the middle
Willow boughs criss-cross and big stones,
That the bees may have plenty of bridges to stand on and dry their
    wings
At the summer sun, in case a shower has caught them loitering
Or a gust of east wind ducked them suddenly in the water.

Green spurge-laurel should grow round about, wild thyme that perfumes
The air, masses of savory rich-breathing, and violet beds
Sucked the channelled stream.
　　Now for the hive itself. Remember, whether you make it
By stitching concave bark or weaving tough withies together,
To give it a narrow doorway: for winter grips and freezes
The honey, and summer's melting heat runs it off to waste.
Either extreme is feared by the bees. It is not for fun
That they're so keen on caulking with wax the draughty chinks
In their roof, and stuff the rim of their hive with flowery pollen,
Storing up for this very job a glue they have gathered
Stickier than bird-lime or pitch from Anatolia. . . .
　　For the rest, when the golden sun has driven winter to ground
And opened up all the leagues of the sky in summer light,
Over the glades and woodlands at once they love to wander
And suck the shining flowers and delicate sip the streams.
Sweet then is their strange delight
As they cherish their children, their nestlings: then with craftsmanship they
Hammer out the fresh wax and mould the tacky honey.

Italy, 1st century B.C.
Trans. from the Latin by
C. Day Lewis

Kuroyanagi Shōha

A heavy cart rumbles,
And from the grass
Flutters a butterfly.

Japan, 18th century
Trans. Bownas & Thwaite

Adlestrop

Edward Thomas

Yes. I remember Adlestrop—
The name, because one afternoon
Of heat the express-train drew up there
Unwontedly. It was late June.

The steam hissed. Someone cleared his throat.
No one left and no one came
On the bare platform. What I saw
Was Adlestrop—only the name

And willows, willow-herb, and grass,
And meadowsweet, and haycocks dry,
No whit less still and lonely fair
Than the high cloudlets in the sky.

And for that minute a blackbird sang
Close by, and round him, mistier,
Farther and farther, all the birds
Of Oxfordshire and Gloucestershire.

England, 20th century

Late Summer

Kinoshita Yūji

The pumpkin tendrils creep
Along the station platform.
A ladybird peeps
From a chink in the half-closed flowers.

A stopping train comes in.
No one gets on, or off.

On the millet stalk
Growing by the railing
The young ticket-man
Rests his clippers.

Japan, 20th century
Trans. Bownas & Thwaite

In the Mountains on a Summer Day

Li Po

Gently I stir a white feather fan,
With open shirt sitting in a green wood.
I take off my cap and hang it on a jutting stone;
A wind from the pine-trees trickles on my bare head.

China, 8th century
Trans. Arthur Waley

The Shower

Henry Vaughan

Waters above! Eternal Springs!
The dew that silvers the Dove's wings!
O welcome, welcome, to the sad:
Give dry dust drink, drink that makes glad!
Many fair evenings, many flowers
Sweetened with rich and gentle showers,
Have I enjoyed, and down have run
Many a fine and shining sun;
But never, till this happy hour,
Was blest with such an evening-shower!

England, 17th century

The Rainy Day

Rabindranath Tagore

Sullen clouds are gathering fast over the black fringe
of the forest.

O child, do not go out!

The palm trees in a row by the lake are smiting their
heads against the dismal sky; the crows with their
draggled wings are silent on the tamarind branches, and
the eastern bank of the river is haunted by a deepening
gloom.

Our cow is lowing loud, tied at the fence.

O child, wait here till I bring her into the stall.

Men have crowded into the flooded field to catch the
fishes as they escape from the overflowing ponds; the
rain-water is running in rills through the narrow lanes
like a laughing boy who has run away from his mother
to tease her.

Listen, someone is shouting for the boatman at the
ford.

O child, the daylight is dim, and the crossing at the
ferry is closed.

The sky seems to ride fast upon the madly rushing
rain; the water in the river is loud and impatient;
women have hastened home early from the Ganges with
their filled pitchers.

The evening lamps must be made ready.

O child, do not go out!

The road to the market is desolate, the lane to the
river is slippery. The wind is roaring and struggling
among the bamboo branches like a wild beast tangled
in a net.

India, 20th century

Rain on Castle Island

Kitahara Hakushū

Rain:
Grey, rat-grey rain
On Castle Island shore;

Rain:
Is it pearls or
Evening mist, or my tears?

A boat
Puts out—my man's
Boat, sail and mast dripping.

Boats
Moved by oars; oars
By songs; songs by the bos'n's mood.

Rain
From cloud-grey sky.
Boat bobbing, sail distant, dim.

Japan, 20th century
Trans. Bownas & Thwaite

The Rainbow

D. H. Lawrence

Even the rainbow has a body
made of the drizzling rain
and is an architecture of glistening atoms
built up, built up.
Yet you can't lay your hand on it
nay, nor even your mind.

England, 20th century

Mist

Andrew Young

Rain, do not fall
Nor rob this mist at all,
That is my only cell and abbey wall.

Wind, wait to blow
And let the thick mist grow,
That fills the rose-cup with a whiter glow.

Mist, deepen still
And the low valley fill:
You hide but taller trees, a higher hill.

Still, mist, draw close;
These gain by what they lose,
The taller trees and hill, the whiter rose.

All else begone,
And leave me here alone
To tread this mist where earth and sky are one.

Scotland, 20th century

Karai Senryū

Sheltering from the rain,
The words on the notice
Are learnt off pat.

Japan, 18th century
Trans. Bownas & Thwaite

119

An Enjoyable Evening in the Village
near the Lake

Lin Ho Ching

A white crow flies from the fairyland.
The mountain's shadow is reflected in the transparent
    water.
In the pale bamboo thicket a dog starts barking.
The busy boatmen return in a group.
The rippling waves are playing with the moonlight.
There floats a bird like fine smoke from the forest.
From the nearby temple sounds the gong.
Suddenly my door shuts.

China, 10th century
Trans. Max Perleberg

Chamber Music (1)

James Joyce

Strings in the earth and air
    Make music sweet;
Strings by the river where
    The willows meet.

There's music along the river
    For Love wanders there,
Pale flowers on his mantle,
    Dark leaves on his hair.

All softly playing,
    With head to the music bent,
And fingers straying
    Upon an instrument.

Ireland, 20th century

from The Prelude

William Wordsworth

One summer evening (led by her) I found
A little boat tied to a willow tree
Within a rocky cove, its usual home.
Straight I unloosed her chain, and stepping in
Pushed from the shore. It was an act of stealth
And troubled pleasure, nor without the voice
Of mountain-echoes did my boat move on;
Leaving behind her still, on either side,
Small circles glittering idly in the moon,
Until they melted all into one track
Of sparkling light. But now, like one who rows,
Proud of his skill, to reach a chosen point
With an unswerving line, I fixed my view
Upon the summit of a craggy ridge,
The horizon's utmost boundary; far above
Was nothing but the stars and the grey sky.
She was an elfin pinnace; lustily
I dipped my oars into the silent lake,
And, as I rose upon the stroke, my boat
Went heaving through the water like a swan;
When, from behind that craggy steep till then
The horizon's bound, a huge peak, black and huge,
As if with voluntary power instinct,
Upreared its head. I struck and struck again,
And growing still in stature the grim shape
Towered up between me and the stars, and still,
For so it seemed, with purpose of its own
And measured motion like a living thing,
Strode after me. With trembling oars I turned,
And through the silent water stole my way
Back to the covert of the willow tree;
There in her mooring-place I left my bark,—
And through the meadows homeward went, in grave

And serious mood; but after I had seen
That spectacle, for many days, my brain
Worked with a dim and undetermined sense
Of unknown modes of being; o'er my thoughts
There hung a darkness, call it solitude
Or blank desertion. No familiar shapes
Remained, no pleasant images of trees,
Of sea or sky, no colours of green fields;
But huge and mighty forms, that do not live
Like living men, moved slowly through the mind
By day, and were a trouble to my dreams.

England, 19th century

On Eastnor Knoll

John Masefield

Silent are the woods, and the dim green boughs are
Hushed in the twilight; yonder, in the path through
The apple orchard, is a tired plough-boy
Calling the cows home.

A bright white star blinks, the pale moon rounds, but
Still the red, lurid wreckage of the sunset
Smoulders in smoky fire, and burns on
The misty hill-tops.

Ghostly it grows, and darker, the burning
Fades into smoke, and now the gusty oaks are
A silent army of phantoms thronging
A land of shadows.

England, 20th century

River Moons

Carl Sandburg

The double moon,
   one on the high backdrop of the west,
   one on the curve of the river face,
The sky moon of fire
   and the river moon of water,
   I am taking these home in a basket,
   hung on an elbow,
   such a teeny-weeny elbow,
   in my head.
I saw them last night,
   a cradle moon, two horns of a moon,
   such an early hopeful moon,
   such a child's moon
   for all young hearts
   to make a picture of.
The river—I remember this like a picture—
   the river was the upper twist
   of a written question mark.
I know now it takes
   many many years to write a river,
   a twist of water asking a question.
And white stars moved when the moon moved,
   and one red star kept burning,
   and the Big Dipper was almost overhead.

U.S.A., 20th century

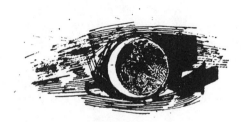

The Unending Sky

John Masefield

I could not sleep for thinking of the sky,
  The unending sky, with all its million suns
Which turn their planets everlastingly
  In nothing, where the fire-haired comet runs.
If I could sail that nothing, I should cross
  Silence and emptiness with dark stars passing;
Then, in the darkness, see a point of gloss
  Burn to a glow, and glare, and keep amassing,
And rage into a sun with wandering planets,
  And drop behind; and then, as I proceed,
See his last light upon his last moon's granites
  Die to a dark that would be night indeed:
Night where my soul might sail a million years
In nothing, not even Death, not even tears.

England, 20th century

The Candle Indoors

Gerard Manley Hopkins

Some candle clear burns somewhere I come by.
I muse at how its being puts blissful back
With yellowy moisture mild night's blear-all black,
Or to-fro tender trambeams truckle at the eye.
By that window what task what fingers ply,
I plod wondering, a-wanting, just for lack
Of answer the eagerer a-wanting Jessy or Jack
There/God to aggrándise, God to glorify.—

124

Come you indoors, come home; your fading fire
Mend first and vital candle in close heart's vault:
You there are master, do your own desire;
What hinders? Are you beam-blind, yet to a fault
In a neighbour deft-handed? are you that liar
And, cast by conscience out, spendsavour salt?

England, 19th century

from A Midsummer Night's Dream

William Shakespeare

Now the hungry lion roars,
   And the wolf behowls the moon;
     Whilst the heavy ploughman snores,
     All with weary task foredone.
Now the wasted brands do glow,
   Whilst the screech-owl, screeching loud,
Puts the wretch, that lies in woe,
   In remembrance of a shroud.
Now it is the time of night,
   That the graves, all gaping wide,
Every one lets forth his sprite,
   In the church-way paths to glide:
And we fairies, that do run
   By the triple Hecate's team,
From the presence of the sun,
   Following darkness like a dream,
Now are frolic; not a mouse
Shall disturb this hallowed house:
I am sent, with broom before,
To sweep the dust behind the door.

England, 16th century

Hurrahing in Harvest

Gerard Manley Hopkins

Summer ends now; now, barbarous in beauty, the stooks arise
  Around; up above, what wind-walks! what lovely behaviour
  Of silk-sack clouds! has wilder, wilful-wavier
Meal-drift moulded ever and melted across skies?

I walk, I lift up, I lift up heart, eyes,
  Down all that glory in the heavens to glean our Saviour;
  And, éyes, heárt, what looks, what lips yet gave you a
Rapturous love's greeting of realer, of rounder replies?

And the azurous hung hills are his world-wielding shoulder
  Majestic—as a stallion stalwart, very-violet-sweet!—
These things, these things were here and but the beholder
  Wanting; which two when they once meet,
The heart réars wíngs bold and bolder
  And hurls for him, O half hurls earth for him off under his feet.

England, 19th century

126

from Windsor Forest

Alexander Pope

See! from the brake the whirring pheasant springs,
And mounts exulting on triumphant wings:
Short is his joy; he feels the fiery wound,
Flutters in blood, and panting beats the ground.
Ah! what avail his glossy, varying dyes,
His purple crest, and scarlet-circled eyes,
The vivid green his shining plumes unfold,
His painted wings, and breast that flames with gold?

England, 18th century

Season

Wole Soyinka

Rust is ripeness, rust
And the wilted corn-plume;
Pollen is mating-time when swallows
Weave a dance
Of feathered arrows
Thread corn-stalks in winged
Streaks of light. And, we loved to hear
Spliced phrases of the wind, to hear
Rasps in the field, where corn leaves
Pierce like bamboo slivers.

Now, garnerers we,
Awaiting rust on tassels, draw
Long shadows from the dusk, wreathe
Dry thatch in wood smoke. Laden stalks
Ride the germ's decay—we await
The promise of the rust.

Nigeria, 20th century

The Wasps' Nest

George MacBeth

All day to the loose tile behind the parapet
The droning bombers fled: in the wet gutter
Belly-upwards the dead were lying, numbered
By October cold. And now the bloat Queen,
Sick-orange, with wings draped, and feelers trailing,
Like Helen combing her hair, posed on the ledge
Twenty feet above the traffic. I watched, just a foot
From her eyes, very glad of the hard glass parting
My pressed human nose from her angry sting
And her heavy power to warm the cold future
Sunk in unfertilised eggs. And I thought: if I reached
And inched this window open, and cut her in half
With my unclasped pen-knife, I could exterminate
An unborn generation. All next summer,
If she survives, the stepped roof will swarm
With a jam of striped fighters. Therefore, this winter
In burning sulphur in their dug-out hangars
All the bred wasps must die. Unless I kill her.
So I balanced assassination with genocide
As the queen walked on the ledge, a foot from my eyes
In the last sun of the year, the responsible man
With a cold nose, who knew that he must kill,
Coming to no sure conclusion, nor anxious to come.

England, 20th century

Riding at Daybreak

Sun Yün Fêng

Not a man is stirring
In the early light,
As my horse trots
Through the rustling yellow leaves.

The pale waning moon
Fades slowly in the dawn,
And a temple bell calls
Through the frosty air.

Far off,
Where forest trees loom through the mist,
A mountain torrent
Rushes down its stony bed.

China, Ch'ing dynasty
Trans. Henry H. Hart

Psalm of Those Who Go Forth Before Daylight

Carl Sandburg

The policeman buys shoes slow and careful; the teamster
buys gloves slow and careful; they take care of their
feet and hands; they live on their feet and hands.

The milkman never argues; he works alone and no one speaks
to him; the city is asleep when he is on the job; he puts
a bottle on six hundred porches and calls it a day's work;
he climbs two hundred wooden stairways; two horses
are company for him; he never argues.

The rolling-mill men and the sheet-steel men are brothers of
  cinders; they empty cinders out of their shoes after the
  day's work; they ask their wives to fix burnt holes in the
  knees of their trousers; their necks and ears are covered
  with a smut; they scour their necks and ears; they are
  brothers of cinders.

U.S.A., 20th century

'Blackie, The Electric Rembrandt'

Thom Gunn

We watch through the shop-front while
Blackie draws stars—an equal

concentration on his and
the youngster's faces. The hand

is steady and accurate;
but the boy does not see it

for his eyes follow the point
that touches (quick, dark movement!)

a virginal arm beneath
his rolled sleeve: he holds his breath.

... Now that it is finished, he
hands a few bills to Blackie

and leaves with a bandage on
his arm, under which gleam ten

stars, hanging in a blue thick
cluster. Now he is starlike.

England, 20th century

Auto Wreck

Karl Shapiro

Its quick soft silver bell beating, beating,
And down the dark one ruby flare
Pulsing out red light like an artery,
The ambulance at top speed floating down
Past beacons and illuminated clocks
Wings in a heavy curve, dips down,
And brakes speed, entering the crowd.
The doors leap open, emptying light;
Stretchers are laid out, the mangled lifted
And stowed into the little hospital.
Then the bell, breaking the hush, tolls once,
And the ambulance with its terrible cargo
Rocking, slightly rocking, moves away,
As the doors, an afterthought, are closed.

We are deranged, walking among the cops
Who sweep glass and are large and composed.
One is still making notes under the light.
One with a bucket douches ponds of blood
Into the street and gutter.
One hangs lanterns on the wrecks that cling,
Empty husks of locusts, to iron poles.

Our throats were tight as tourniquets,
Our feet were bound with splints, but now,
Like convalescents intimate and gauche,
We speak through sickly smiles and warn
With the stubborn saw of common sense,
The grim joke and the banal resolution.
The traffic moves around with care,

But we remain, touching a wound
That opens to our richest horror.

Already old, the question Who shall die?
Becomes unspoken Who is innocent?
For death in war is done by hands;
Suicide has cause and stillbirth, logic;
And cancer, simple as a flower, blooms.

But this invites the occult mind,
Cancels our physics with a sneer,
And spatters all we knew of denouement
Across the expedient and wicked stones.

U.S.A., 20th century

e. e. cummings

nobody loses all the time

i had an uncle named
Sol who was a born failure and
nearly everybody said he should have gone
into vaudeville perhaps because my Uncle Sol could
sing McCann He Was A Diver on Xmas Eve like Hell Itself which
may or may not account for the fact that my Uncle

Sol indulged in that possibly most inexcusable
of all to use a highfalootin phrase
luxuries that is or to
wit farming and be
it needlessly
added

my Uncle Sol's farm
failed because the chickens
ate the vegetables so
my Uncle Sol had a
chicken farm till the
skunks ate the chickens when

my Uncle Sol
had a skunk farm but
the skunks caught cold and
died and so
my Uncle Sol imitated the
skunks in a subtle manner

or by drowning himself in the watertank
but somebody who'd given my Uncle Sol a Victor
Victrola and records while he lived presented to
him upon the auspicious occasion of his decease a
scrumptious not to mention splendiferous funeral with
tall boys in black gloves and flowers and everything and

i remember we all cried like the Missouri
when my Uncle Sol's coffin lurched because
somebody pressed a button
(and down went
my Uncle
Sol

and started a worm farm)

U.S.A., 20th century

133

Circles

Carl Sandburg

The white man drew a small circle in the sand
   and told the red man,
   'This is what the Indian knows,'
   and drawing a big circle around the small one,
   'This is what the white man knows.'

The Indian took the stick
   and swept an immense ring around both circles:
   'This is where the white man and the red man
   know nothing.'

U.S.A., 20th century

Telephone Conversation

Wole Soyinka

The price seemed reasonable, location
Indifferent. The landlady swore she lived
Off premises. Nothing remained
But self-confession. 'Madam,' I warned,
'I hate a wasted journey—I am African.'
Silence. Silenced transmission of
Pressurized good-breeding. Voice, when it came,
Lipstick-coated, long gold-rolled
Cigarette-holder pipped. Caught I was, foully.
'HOW DARK?'...I had not misheard...'ARE YOU LIGHT
OR VERY DARK?' Button B. Button A. Stench
Of rancid breath of public hide-and-speak.

Red booth. Red pillar box. Red double-tiered
Omnibus squelching tar. It *was* real! Shamed
By ill-mannered silence, surrender
Pushed dumbfounded to beg simplification.
Considerate she was, varying the emphasis—
'ARE YOU DARK? OR VERY LIGHT?' Revelation came.
'You mean—like plain or milk chocolate?'
Her assent was clinical, crushing in its light
Impersonality. Rapidly, wave-length adjusted,
I chose. 'West African sepia'—and as afterthought,
'Down in my passport.' Silence for spectroscopic
Flight of fancy, till truthfulness clanged her accent
Hard on the mouthpiece. 'WHAT'S THAT?' conceding
'DON'T KNOW WHAT THAT IS.' 'Like brunette.'
'THAT'S DARK, ISN'T IT?' 'Not altogether.
Facially, I am brunette, but madam, you should see
The rest of me. Palm of my hand, soles of my feet
Are a peroxide blonde. Friction, caused—
Foolishly madam   by sitting down, has turned
My bottom raven black—One moment, madam!'—sensing
Her receiver rearing on the thunderclap
About my ears—'Madam,' I pleaded, 'wouldn't you rather
See for yourself?'

Nigeria, 20th century

135

The School Boy

William Blake

I love to rise in a summer morn
When the birds sing on every tree;
The distant huntsman winds his horn,
And the sky-lark sings with me.
O! what sweet company.

But to go to school in a summer morn,
O! it drives all joy away;
Under a cruel eye outworn,
The little ones spend the day
In sighing and dismay.

Ah! then at times I drooping sit,
And spend many an anxious hour,
Nor in my book can I take delight,
Nor sit in learning's bower,
Worn through with the dreary shower.

How can the bird that is born for joy
Sit in a cage and sing?
How can a child, when fears annoy,
But droop his tender wing,
And forget his youthful spring?

O! father and mother, if buds are nipped
And blossoms blown away,
And if the tender plants are stripped
Of their joy in the springing day,
By sorrow and care's dismay,

How shall the summer arise in joy,
Or the summer fruits appear?
Or how shall we gather what griefs destroy,
Or bless the mellowing year,
When the blasts of winter appear?

England, 18th century

Schoolmaster

Yevgeny Yevtushenko

The window gives onto the white trees.
The master looks out of it at the trees,
for a long time, he looks for a long time
out through the window at the trees,
breaking his chalk slowly in one hand.
And it's only the rules of long division.
And he's forgotten the rules of long division.
Imagine not remembering long division!
A mistake on the blackboard, a mistake.
We watch him with a different attention
needing no one to hint to us about it,
there's more than difference in this attention.
The schoolmaster's wife has gone away,
we do not know where she has gone to,
we do not know why she has gone,
what we know is his wife has gone away.

His clothes are neither new nor in the fashion;
wearing the suit which he always wears
and which is neither new nor in the fashion
the master goes downstairs to the cloakroom.
He fumbles in his pocket for a ticket.
'What's the matter? Where is that ticket?
Perhaps I never picked up my ticket.
Where is the thing?' Rubbing his forehead.
'Oh, here it is. I'm getting old.
Don't argue auntie dear, I'm getting old.
You can't do much about getting old.'
We hear the door below creaking behind him.

The window gives onto the white trees.
The trees there are high and wonderful,
but they are not why we are looking out.

137

We look in silence at the schoolmaster.
He has a bent back and clumsy walk,
he moves without defences, clumsily,
worn out I ought to have said, clumsily.
Snow falling on him softly through silence
turns him to white under the white trees.
He whitens into white like the trees.
A little longer will make him so white
we shall not see him in the whitened trees.

U.S.S.R., 20th century
Trans. Milner-Gulland & Levi

Waiting

James Kirkup

I wait with a pencil in my hand
Beside the morning's empty page,
Not hoping for a sign, but waiting
For a word that will engage
The stillness with a sound
Of its own making.

Outside the paper room
The children in the playground kill
The summer with their cries.
I look out at the sunny hill
Of sky, but cannot catch the words they scream
To give their spirits ease.

If I, too, could give a shout
Of fear or pleasure, I could play
Myself into their endless game.
But I stand outside their day.
The dumb words are fastened in my throat,
And will not come.

England, 20th century

Dansui

Even before His Majesty,
The scarecrow does not remove
His plaited hat.

Japan, 17th century
Trans. R. H. Blyth

Envy

Yevgeny Yevtushenko

I envy.
        This secret
I have not revealed before.
I know
        there is somewhere a boy
whom I greatly envy.
I envy
        the way he fights;
I myself was never so guileless and bold.
I envy
        the way he laughs—
as a boy I could never laugh like that.
He always walks about with bumps and bruises;
I've always been better combed,
                                intact.
He will not miss
                all those passages in books
I've missed.
                Here he is stronger too.
He will be more blunt and harshly honest,
forgiving no evil for any good it may bring;
and where I'd dropped my pen:
                        'It isn't worth it . . .'

139

he'd assert:
                    'It's worth it!'
                                    and pick up the pen.
If he can't unravel a knot,
                    he'll cut it through,
where I can neither unravel a knot,
                                    nor cut it through.
Once he falls in love,
                    he won't fall out of it,
where I keep falling in
                    and out of love.
I'll hide my envy.
                    Start to smile.
I'll pretend to be a simple soul:
'Someone has to smile;
someone has to live in a different way . . .'
But much as I tried to persuade myself of this,
repeating:
                    'To each man his fate . . .'
I can't forget there is somewhere a boy
who will achieve far more than I.

U.S.S.R., 20th century
Trans. George Reavey

from Burning

John Muir on Mt Ritter

Gary Snyder

After scanning its face again and again,
I began to scale it, picking my holds
With intense caution. About halfway
To the top, I was suddenly brought to
A dead stop, with arms outspread
Clinging close to the face of the rock
Unable to move hand or foot
Either up or down. My doom
Appeared fixed. I MUST fall.

There would be a moment of
Bewilderment, and then,
A lifeless rumble down the cliff
To the glacier below.
My mind seemed to fill with a
Stifling smoke. This terrible eclipse
Lasted only a moment, when life blazed
Forth again with preternatural clearness.
I seemed suddenly to become possessed
Of a new sense. My trembling muscles
Became firm again, every rift and flaw in
The rock was seen as through a microscope,
My limbs moved with a positiveness and precision
With which I seemed to have
Nothing at all to do.

U.S.A., 20th century

A Correct Compassion

James Kirkup

*To Mr Philip Allison, after watching him perform a Mitral
Stenosis Valvulotomy in the General Infirmary at Leeds.*

Cleanly, sir, you went to the core of the matter.
Using the purest kind of wit, a balance of belief and
    art,
You with a curious nervous elegance laid bare
The root of life, and put your finger on its beating
    heart.

The glistening theatre swarms with eyes, and hands,
    and eyes.
On green-clothed tables, ranks of instruments
    transmit a sterile gleam.
The masks are on, and no unnecessary smile betrays
A certain tension, true concomitant of calm.

Here we communicate by looks, though words,
Too, are used, as in continuous historic present
You describe our observations and your deeds.'
All gesture is reduced to its result, an instrument.

She who does not know she is a patient lies
Within a tent of green, and sleeps without a sound
Beneath the lamps, and the reflectors that devise
Illuminations probing the profoundest wound.

A calligraphic master, improvising, you invent
The first incision, and no poet's hesitation
Before his snow-blank page mars your intent:
The flowing stroke is drawn like an uncalculated
    inspiration.

A garland of flowers unfurls across the painted
    flesh.
With quick precision the arterial forceps click.
Yellow threads are knotted with a simple flourish.
Transfused, the blood preserves its rose, though it is
    sick.

Meters record the blood, measure heart-beats,
    control the breath.
Hieratic gesture: scalpel bares a creamy rib; with
    pincer knives
The bone is quietly clipped, and lifted out. Beneath,
The pink, black-mottled lung like a revolted creature
    heaves,

Collapses; as if by extra fingers is neatly held aside
By two ordinary egg-beaters, kitchen tools that curve
Like extraordinary hands. Heart, laid bare, silently
    beats. It can hide
No longer, yet is not revealed.—'A local anaesthetic
    in the cardiac nerve.'

Now, in firm hands that quiver with a careful
        strength,
Your knife feels through the heart's transparent skin;
        at first,
Inside the pericardium, slit down half its length,
The heart, black-veined, swells like a fruit about to
        burst,

But goes on beating, love's poignant image bleeding
        at the dart
Of a more grievous passion, as a bird, dreaming of
        flight, sleeps on
Within its leafy cage.—'It generally upsets the heart
A bit, though not unduly, when I make the first
        injection.'

Still, still the patient sleeps, and still the speaking
        heart is dumb.
The watchers breathe an air far sweeter, rarer than
        the room's.
The cold walls listen. Each in his own blood hears the
        drum
She hears, tented in green, unfathomable folds.

'I make a purse-string suture here, with a reserve
Suture, which I must make first, and deeper,
As a safeguard, should the other burst. In the cardiac
        nerve
I inject again a local anaesthetic. Could we have fresh
        towels to cover

All these adventitious ones. Now can you all see?
When I put my finger inside the valve, there may be a
        lot
Of blood, and it may come out with quite a bang. But
        I let it flow,
In case there are any clots, to give the heart a good
        clean-out.

143

Now can you give me every bit of light you've got.'
We stand on the benches, peering over his shoulder.
The lamp's intensest rays are concentrated on an
    inmost heart.
Someone coughs.—'If you have to cough, you will do
    it outside this theatre.'
                       '—Yes, sir.'

'How's she breathing, Doug.? Do you feel quite
    happy?'—
             —'Yes fairly
Happy.'—'Now. I am putting my finger in the
    opening of the valve
I can only get the tip of my finger in.—It's gradually
Giving way.—I'm inside.—No clots.—I can feel the
    valve

Breathing freely now around my finger, and the heart
    working.
Not too much blood. It opened very nicely.
I should say that anatomically speaking
This is a perfect case.—Anatomically.

For of course, anatomy is not physiology.'
We find we breathe again, and hear the surgeon hum.
Outside, in the street, a car starts up. The heart
    regularly
Thunders.—'I do not stitch up the pericardium.

It is not necessary.' For this is imagination's other
    place,
Where only necessary things are done, with the
    supreme and grave
Dexterity that ignores technique; with proper grace
Informing a correct compassion, that performs its
    love, and makes it live.

England, 20th century

After Ever Happily

or

The Princess and the Woodcutter★

Ian Serraillier

And they both lived happily ever after . . .
The wedding was held in the palace. Laughter
Rang to the roof as a loosened rafter
Crashed down and squashed the chamberlain flat—
And how the wedding guests chuckled at that!
'You, with your horny indelicate hands,
Who drop your haitches and call them 'ands,
Who cannot afford to buy her a dress,
How dare you presume to pinch our princess—
Miserable woodcutter, uncombed, unwashed!'
Were the chamberlain's words (before he was squashed).
'Take her,' said the Queen, who had a soft spot
For woodcutters. 'He's strong and he's handsome. Why
    not?'
'What rot!' said the King, but he dare not object;
The Queen wore the trousers—that's as you'd expect.
Said the chamberlain, usually meek and inscrutable,
'A princess and a woodcutter? The match is unsuitable.'
Her dog barked its welcome again and again,
As they splashed to the palace through puddles of rain.
And the princess sighed, 'Till the end of my life!'
'Darling,' said the woodcutter, 'will you be my wife?'
He knew all his days he could love no other,
So he nursed her to health with some help from his
    mother,
And lifted her, horribly hurt, from her tumble.
A woodcutter, watching, saw the horse stumble.
As she rode through the woods, a princess in her prime
On a dapple-grey horse . . . Now, to finish my rhyme,
I'll start it properly: Once upon a time—

England, 20th century

★ This is a love story from the Middle Ages. The poet obviously knew his subject
backwards.

145

Young Beichan

Anon.

In London was Young Beichan born,
    He longed strange countries for to see;
But he was ta'en by a savage Moor
    Who handled him right cruelly.

For he viewed the fashions of that land,
    Their way of worship viewèd he;
But to Mahound or Termagant
    Would Beichan never bend a knee.

So through every shoulder they've bored a bore,
    And through every bore they've putten a tree,
And they have made him trail the wine
    And spices on his fair body.

They've casten him in a dungeon deep,
    Where he could neither hear nor see;
And fed him on nought but bread and water
    Till he for hunger's like to die.

This Moor he had but ae daughter,
    Her name was callèd Susie Pye,
And every day as she took the air
    She heard Young Beichan sadly cry:

'My hounds they all run masterless,
    My hawks they fly from tree to tree,
My youngest brother will heir my lands;
    Fair England again I'll never see!

'O were I free as I hae been,
    And my ship swimming once more on sea,
I'd turn my face to fair England
    And sail no more to a strange country!'

Young Beichan's song for thinking on
    All night she never closed her e'e;
She's stown the keys from her father's head
    Wi' mickle gold and white money.

And she has opened the prison doors:
    I wot she opened twa or three
Ere she could come Young Beichan at,
    He was locked up so curiously.

'O hae ye any lands or rents,
    Or cities in your own country,
Could free you out of prison strong
    And could maintain a lady free?'—

'O London city is my own,
    And other cities twa or three;
I'll give them all to the lady fair
    That out of prison will set me free.'

O she has bribed her father's men
    Wi' mickle gold and white money,
She's gotten the keys of the prison strong,
    And she has set Young Beichan free.

She's fed him upon the good spice-cake,
    The Spanish wine and the malvoisie;
She's broken a ring from off her finger
    And to Beichan half of it gave she.

'Go set your foot on good shipboard,
    And haste you back to your own country,
But before that seven years has an end,
    Come back again, love, and marry me.'

It was long or seven years had an end
    She longed full sore her love to see;
So she's set her foot on good ship-board
    And turned her back on her own country.

She's sailèd east, she's sailèd west,
    She's sailèd all across the sea,
And when she came to fair England
    The bells were ringing merrily.

'O whose are a' yon flock o' sheep?
    And whose are a' yon flock o' kye?
And whose are a' yon pretty castles,
    That I so often do pass by?'

'O they are a' Lord Beichan's sheep,
    And they are a' Lord Beichan's kye,
And they are a' Lord Beichan's castles
    That you so often do pass by.

'O there's a wedding in yonder ha',
    Has lasted thirty days and three;
Lord Beichan will not bed wi' his bride
    For love of one that's 'yond the sea.'

When she came to Young Beichan's gate
    She tirlèd softly at the pin;
So ready was the proud portèr
    To open and let this lady in.

'Is this Young Beichan's gates?' she says,
    'Or is that noble lord within?'—
'He's up the stairs wi' his bonny bride,
    For this is the day o' his weddin'.'—

'O has he taken a bonny bride,
    And has he clean forgotten me?'
And sighing said that lady gay,
    'I wish I were in my own country!'

She's putten her hand in her pockèt
    And gi'en the porter guineas three;
Says, 'Take ye that, ye proud portèr,
    And bid the bridegroom speak with me.'

And she has ta'en her gay gold ring,
    That with her love she brake so free;
Says, 'Gie him that, ye proud portèr,
    And bid the bridegroom speak with me.'

O when the porter came up the stair,
    He's kneelèd low upon his knee:
'Won up, won up, ye proud portèr,
    And what makes a' this courtesy?'—

'O I've been porter at your gates
    I'm sure this thirty years and three,
But there is a lady stands thereat
    The fairest I did ever see.'

It's out then spake the bride's mother,
    —Aye, and an angry woman was she—
'Ye might have excepted our bonny bride,
    And twa or three of our company.'

'My dame, your daughter's fair enough,
    And aye the fairer mote she be!
But the fairest time that ever she was,
    She'll no compare wi' this lady.

'For on every finger she has a ring,
  And on the mid-finger she has three,
And as mickle gold she has on her brow
  'Would buy an earldom o' land to me.

'And this golden ring that's broken in twa,
  She sends the half o' this golden ring,
And bids you speak with a lady fair,
  That out o' prison did you bring.'

Then up and started Young Beichan
  And sware so loud by Our Lady,
'It can be none but Susie Pye,
  That has come over the sea to me!'

O quickly ran he down the stair,
  Of fifteen steps he made but three;
He's ta'en his bonny love in his arms
  And kissed and kissed her tenderly.

'O have ye ta'en another bride,
  And have ye quite forsaken me?
And have ye clean forgotten her
  That gave you life and liberty?'

She's lookèd over her left shoulder
  To hide the tears stood in her e'e;
'Now fare-thee-well, Young Beichan,' she says—
  'I'll strive to think no more on thee.'

'O never, never, Susie Pye,
  For surely this can never be,
That ever I shall wed but her
  That's done and dreed so much for me!'

Then up bespake the bride's mother—
    She never was heard to speak so free:
'Ye'll not forsake my only daughter,
    Though Susie Pye has crossed the sea.'

'Take home, take home your daughter, madam,
    She's never a bit the worse for me;
For saving a kiss of her bonny lips
    Of your daughter's body I am free.'

He's ta'en her by the milk-white hand
    And led her to yon fountain-stone;
He's changed her name from Susie Pye
    And called her his bonny love Lady Joan.

Scotland, trad.

Folk Song from Fukushima

Anon.

Handsome boy!
O for a thread
To haul him over
To my side!

Japan, 17th century
Trans. Bownas & Thwaite

Lord Thomas and Fair Eleanor

Anon.

Lord Thomas he was a bold forester,
The chasener of the King's deer.
Fair Eleanor she was a fair woman;
Lord Thomas he loved her dear.

151

'Oh riddle, oh riddle, dear mother,' he said,
'Oh riddle it both as one,
Whether I shall marry fair Ellen or not,
And leave the brown girl alone?'

'The brown girl she've a-got houses and land,
Fair Ellen she've a-got none,
Therefore I charge thee to my blessing
To bring the brown girl home.'

Lord Thomas he went to fair Eleanor's tower.
He knocked so loud on the ring.
There was none so ready as fair Eleanor's self
To let Lord Thomas in.

'What news, what news, Lord Thomas?' she said,
'What news have you brought to me?'
'I've come to invite thee to my wedding
Beneath the sycamore tree.'

'O God forbid, Lord Thomas,' she said,
'That any such thing should be done.
I thought to have been a bride myself,
And you to have been the groom!'

'Oh riddle, oh riddle, dear mother!' she said,
'Oh riddle it both as one,
Whether I go to Lord Thomas's wedding,
Or better I stay at home?'

'There's a hundred of thy friends, dear child,
A hundred of thy foes,
Therefore I beg thee with all my blessing
To Lord Thomas's wedding don't go.'

But she dressed herself in her best attire,
Her merry men all in green,
And every town that she went through
They thought she was some queen.

Lord Thomas he took her by the hand,
He led her through the hall,
And he sat her down in the noblest chair
Among the ladies all.

'Is this your bride, Lord Thomas?' she says,
'I'm sure she looks wonderful brown,
When you used to have the fairest young lady
That ever the sun shone on!'

'Despise her not,' Lord Thomas he said,
'Despise her not unto me.
For more do I love your little finger
Than all her whole body.'

This brown girl she had a little pen-knife
Which was both long and sharp.
And betwixt the long ribs and the short
She pricked fair Eleanor's heart.

'Oh what is the matter?' Lord Thomas he said.
'Oh can you not very well see?
Can you not see my own heart's blood
Come trickling down my knee?'

Lord Thomas's sword is hung by his side,
As he walked up and down the hall,
And he took off the brown girl's head from her
    shoulders,
And he flung it against the wall.

He put the handle to the ground,
The sword into his heart.
No sooner did three lovers meet,
No sooner did they part.

Lord Thomas was buried in the church,
Fair Eleanor in the choir,
And out of her bosom there grew a red rose,
And out of Lord Thomas a briar.

And it grew till it reached the church steeple top,
Where it could grow no higher,
And there it entwined like a true lover's knot
For all true loves to admire.

England, date unknown
Sung by Mrs Pond, Shepton Beauchamp, Somerset

The Cap and Bells

W. B. Yeats

The jester walked in the garden:
The garden had fallen still;
He bade his soul rise upward
And stand on her window-sill.

It rose in a straight blue garment,
When owls began to call:
It had grown wise-tongued by thinking
Of a quiet and light footfall;

But the young queen would not listen;
She rose in her pale night-gown;
She drew in the heavy casement
And pushed the latches down.

He bade his heart go to her,
When the owls called out no more;
In a red and quivering garment
It sang to her through the door.

It had grown sweet-tongued by dreaming
Of a flutter of flower-like hair;
But she took up her fan from the table
And waved it off on the air.

'I have cap and bells,' he pondered,
'I will send them to her and die';
And when the morning whitened
He left them where she went by.

She laid them upon her bosom,
Under a cloud of her hair,
And her red lips sang them a love-song
Till stars grew out of the air.

She opened her door and her window,
And the heart and the soul came through,
To her right hand came the red one,
To her left hand came the blue.

They set up a noise like crickets,
A chattering wise and sweet,
And her hair was a folded flower
And the quiet of love in her feet.

Ireland, 20th century

The Death of Robin Hood

Anon.

When Robin Hood and Little John
   Down a-down, a-down, a-down
   Went o'er yon bank of broom,
Said Robin Hood to Little John,
   'We have shot for many a pound,
   Hey! down a-down, a-down!

'But I am not able to shoot one shot more,
   My proud arrows will not flee;
But I have a cousin lives down below,
   Please God, she will now bleed me.

'I will never eat nor drink,' he said,
   'Nor meat will do me good,
Till I have been to merry Kirkleys
   My veins for to let blood.

'The dame prior is my aunt's daughter,
   And nigh unto my kin;
I know she would do me no harm this day,
   For all the world to win.'

'That I advise not,' said Little John,
   'Master, by the assent of me,
Without half a hundred of your best bowmen
   You take to go with ye.'

'If thou be afeared, thou Little John,
   At home I bid thee be.'
'If you be wroth, my dear master,
   'You shall never hear more of me.'

Now Robin is gone to merry Kirkleys,
  And there he knockèd upon the pin;
Up then rose Dame Priorèss,
  And let good Robin in.

Then Robin gave to Dame Priorèss
  Twenty pounds in gold,
And bade her spend while that did last,
  She should have more when she would.

'Will you please to sit down, cousin Robin,
  And drink some beer with me?'
'No, I will neither eat nor drink
  Till I am blooded by thee.'

Down then came Dame Priorèss,
  Down she came full quick,
With a pair of blood-irons in her hands.
  Were wrappèd all in silk.

'Set a chafing-dish to the fire,' she said,
  'And strip thou up thy sleeve.'
(I hold him but an unwise man
  That will no warning believe.)

She laid the blood-irons to Robin's vein,
  Alack, the more pitỳ!
And pierced the vein, and let out the blood
  That full red was to see.

And first it bled the thick, thick blood.
  And afterwards the thin,
And well then wist good Robin Hood
  Treason there was within.

And there she blooded bold Robin Hood
    While one drop of blood would run;
There he did bleed the live-long day,
    Until the next at noon.

He bethought him then of the casement there,
    Being locked up in the room;
But was so weak, he could not leap,
    He could not get him down.

He bethought him then of his bugle-horn,
    That hung low down to his knee;
He set his horn unto his mouth,
    And blew out weak blasts three.

Then Little John he heard the horn,
    Where he sat under a tree;
'I fear my master is now near dead,
    He blows so wearily.'

Little John is gone to merry Kirkleys,
    As fast as he can dree,
And when he came to merry Kirkleys
    He broke locks two or three.

Until he came bold Robin unto,
    Then he fell on his knee;
'A boon, a boon!' cries Little John,
    'Master, I beg of thee!'

'What is that boon,' said Robin Hood,
    'That thou dost beg of me?'
'It is to burn fair Kirkleys-hall,
    And all their nunnery.'

'Now nay, now nay,' quoth Robin Hood,
   'That boon I'll not grant thee;
I never hurt woman in all my life,
   Nor men in their companỳ.

'I never hurt maid in all my life,
   Nor at my end shall it be,
But give me my bent bow in my hand,
   And a broad arrow I'll let flee;
And where that arrow is taken up
   There shall my grave digged be.

'Lay me a green sod under my head,
   Another at my feet,
And lay my bent bow at my side,
   Which was my music sweet;
And make my grave of gravel and green,
   Which is most right and meet.

'Let me have length and breadth enough,
   And under my head a sod;
That they may say when I am dead,
   "Here lies bold Robin Hood!"'
   Down a-down, a-down, a-down,
   Hey! down a-down, a-down.

England, trad.

Judas

Anon.

It was upon a Maundy Thursday that our Lord
    arose;
Full mild were the words he spake to Judas:
'Judas, thou must to Jerusalem, our meat for to buy,
Thirty pieces of silver thou shalt take with thee.

Thou shalt come far into the broad street, far into
    the broad street;
Some of thy kinsmen there thou must meet.'

He has met with his sister, the wicked woman:
'Judas thou art worthy to be stoned with stone,
Judas, thou art worthy to be stoned with stone,
For the false prophet that thou believest on.'

'Be still, loved sister, lest thy heart break!
Wist my Lord Jesus, full well he would be wreke.'

'Judas, go thou over rock, go thou over stone,
Lay thy head in my bosom, sleep thou anon.'

Soon as Judas from his sleep was awake
Thirty pieces of silver from him were i-take.

He tore his hair, till his head was laved in blood;
The Jews in Jerusalem thought he was mad.

Towards him came the rich Jew that was called
    Pilatus:
'Wilt thou sell the Lord, that is called Jesus.'

'I wad sell my Lord for no kind of good
But it be for the thirty pieces that he entrust to me
    would.'...

In came our Lord, as his apostles sat at meat:
'Why sit ye, apostles, and why need ye eat.
Why sit ye apostles, and why need ye eat
I am bought and sold to-day for our meat.'

Up stood Judas 'Lord, is it I?
I was never in the place when thou spoke evil of me.'

Up stood Peter and spake with all his might:
'Though Pilatus came with ten hundred knights.
Though Pilatus came with ten hundred knights
Yet I will, Lord, for thy love fight.'
'Still be thou, Peter! Well I thee know;
Thou will forsake me thrice ere the cock crow.'

England, 13th century

from The Tragical History of Doctor Faustus

Christopher Marlowe

FAUSTUS: Ah, Faustus,
  Now hast thou but one bare hour to live,
  And then thou must be damned perpetually!
  Stand still, you ever-moving spheres of Heaven,
  That time may cease, and midnight never come;
  Fair Nature's eye, rise, rise again and make
  Perpetual day; or let this hour be but
  A year, a month, a week, a natural day,
  That Faustus may repent and save his soul!
  O lente, lente, currite noctis equi!
  The stars move still, time runs, the clock will strike,
  The Devil will come, and Faustus must be damned.
  Oh, I'll leap up to my God! Who pulls me down?
  See, see, where Christ's blood streams in the firmament!
  One drop would save my soul—half a drop:
      ah, my Christ!

Ah, rend not my heart for naming of my Christ!
Yet will I call on him: Oh spare me, Lucifer!—
Where is it now? 'tis gone; and see where God
Stretcheth out his arm, and bends his ireful brows!
Mountains and hills come, come and fall on me,
And hide me from the heavy wrath of God!
No! no!
Then will I headlong run into the earth;
Earth gape! Oh no, it will not harbour me!
You stars that reigned at my nativity,
Whose influence hath allotted Death and Hell,
Now draw up Faustus like a foggy mist
Into the entrails of yon labouring cloud,
That when you vomit forth into the air,
My limbs may issue from your smoky mouths,
So that my soul may but ascend to Heaven.
   [*The watch strikes.*]
Ah, half the hour is past! 'twill all be past anon!
Oh God!
If thou wilt not have mercy on my soul,
Yet for Christ's sake, whose blood hath ransomed me,
Impose some end to my incessant pain;
Let Faustus live in Hell a thousand years—
A hundred thousand, and at last be saved!
Oh, no end is limited to damnèd souls!
Why wert thou not a creature wanting soul?
Or why is this immortal that thou hast?
Ah, Pythagoras' Metempsychosis! were that true,
This soul should fly from me, and I be changed
Unto some brutish beast! all beasts are happy,
For, when they die,
Their souls are soon dissolved in elements;
But mine must live, still to be plagued in Hell.
Cursed be the parents that engendered me!
No, Faustus: curse thyself: curse Lucifer
That hath deprived thee of the joys of Heaven.

[*The clock strikes twelve.*]
Oh, it strikes, it strikes! Now body, turn to air,
Or Lucifer will bear thee quick to Hell.
  [*Thunder and lightning.*]
Oh, soul be changed into little water-drops,
And fall into the ocean—ne'er be found.
  [*Enter Devils.*]
My God! my God! look not so fierce on me!
Adders and serpents, let me breathe awhile!
Ugly Hell gape not! come not, Lucifer!
I'll burn my books!—Ah, Mephistophilis!
  [*Exeunt Devils with him.*]

England, 16th century

Karai Senryū

Judging from the pictures,
Hell looks the more
Interesting place.

Japan, 18th century
Trans. Bownas & Thwaite

Emily Dickinson

Because I could not stop for Death,
He kindly stopped for me;
The carriage held but just ourselves
And Immortality.

We slowly drove, he knew no haste,
And I had put away
My labour, and my leisure too,
For his civility.

We passed the school where children played
Their lessons scarcely done;
We passed the fields of gazing grain,
We passed the setting sun.

We paused before a house that seemed
A swelling of the ground;
The roof was scarcely visible,
The cornice but a mound.

Since then 'tis centuries; but each
Feels shorter than the day
I first surmised the horses' heads
Were toward eternity.

U.S.A., 19th century

Dives and Lazarus

Anon.

As it fell out upon a day,
  Rich Dives he made a feast,
And he invited all his friends
  And gentry of the best.

Then Lazarus laid him down and down,
  And down at Dives' door;
'Some meat, some drink, brother Dives,
  Bestow upon the poor!'—

'Thou art none of my brother, Lazarus,
  That lies begging at my door;
No meat nor drink will I give thee,
  Nor bestow upon the poor.'

Then Lazarus laid him down and down,
  And down at Dives' wall;
'Some meat, some drink, brother Dives,
  Or with hunger starve I shall!'—

'Thou art none of my brother, Lazarus,
    That lies begging at my wall;
No meat nor drink will I give thee,
    But with hunger starve you shall.'

Then Lazarus laid him down and down,
    And down at Dives' gate;
'Some meat, some drink, brother Dives,
    For Jesus Christ his sake!'—

'Thou art none of my brother, Lazarus,
    That lies begging at my gate;
No meat nor drink will I give thee,
    For Jesus Christ his sake.'

Then Dives sent out his merry men,
    To whip poor Lazarus away;
They had no power to strike a stroke,
    But flung their whips away.

Then Dives sent out his hungry dogs,
    To bite him as he lay;
They had no power to bite at all,
    But lickèd his sores away.

As it fell out upon a day,
    Poor Lazarus sickened and died;
Then came two angels out of heaven
    His soul therein to guide.

'Rise up, rise up, brother Lazarus,
    And go along with me;
For you've a place prepared in heaven,
    To sit on an angel's knee.'

As it fell out upon a day,
  Rich Dives sickened and died;
Then came two serpents out of hell,
  His soul therein to guide.

'Rise up, rise up, brother Dives,
  And go with us to see
A dismal place, prepared in hell,
  To sit on a serpent's knee.'

Then Dives looked up with his eyes,
  And saw poor Lazarus blest;
'Give me one drop of water, brother Lazarus,
  To quench my flaming thirst.

'Oh had I as many years to abide
  As there are blades of grass,
Then there would be an end, but now
  Hell's pains will ne'er be past!

'Oh was I now but alive again,
  The space of one half hour!
Oh that I had my peace secure!
  Then the devil should have no power.'

England, c. 16th century

Death of a Peasant

R. S. Thomas

You remember Davies? He died, you know,
With his face to the wall, as the manner is
Of the poor peasant in his stone croft
On the Welsh hills. I recall the room
Under the slates, and the smirched snow
Of the wide bed in which he lay,
Lonely as an ewe that is sick to lamb
In the hard weather of mid-March.
I remember also the trapped wind
Tearing the curtains, and the wild light's
Frequent hysteria upon the floor,
The bare floor without a rug
Or mat to soften the loud tread
Of neighbours crossing the uneasy boards
To peer at Davies with gruff words
Of meaningless comfort, before they turned
Heartless away from the stale smell
Of death in league with those dank walls.

Wales, 20th century

Elegy for J.F.K.

(November 22nd 1963)

W. H. Auden

Why *then*, why *there*,
Why *thus*, we cry, did he die?
The heavens are silent.

What he was, he was:
What he is fated to become
Depends on us.

Remembering his death,
How we choose to live
Will decide its meaning.

When a just man dies,
Lamentation and praise,
Sorrow and joy, are one.

U.S.A., 20th century

The Dying Child

John Clare

He could not die when trees were green,
  For he loved the time too well.
His little hands, when flowers were seen,
  Were held for the bluebell,
    As he was carried o'er the green.

His eye glanced at the white-nosed bee;
  He knew those children of the Spring:
When he was well and on the lea
  He held one in his hand to sing,
    Which filled his heart with glee.

Infants, the children of the Spring!
  How can an infant die
When butterflies are on the wing,
  Green grass, and such a sky?
    How can they die at Spring?

He held his hands for daisies white,
  And then for violets blue,
And took them all to bed at night
  That in the green fields grew,
    As childhood's sweet delight.

And then he shut his little eyes,
    And flowers would notice not;
Birds' nests and eggs caused no surprise,
    He now no blossoms got!
        Thus met with plaintive sighs.

When Winter came and blasts did sigh,
    And bare were plain and tree,
As he for ease in bed did lie
    His soul seemed with the free,
        He died so quietly.

England, 19th century

'Adieu!'

John Clare

I left the little birds
And the sweet lowing of the herds,
And couldn't find out words,
        Do you see,
To say to them good-bye,
Where the yellowcups do lie;
So heaving a deep sigh,
        Took to sea . . .

England, 19th century

from At the Grave of John Clare

Charles Causley

Walking in the scythed churchyard, around the locked
    church,
Walking among the oaks and snails and mossed
    inscriptions
At first we failed to find the grave.
But a girl said 'There he is: there is John Clare!'

And we stood, silent, by the ridged stone,
A stone of grey cheese.
There were no flowers for the dead ploughman
As the gilt clock fired off the hour,
Only the words:
A poet is born not made. . . .

O Clare! Your poetry clear, translucent
As your lovely name,
I salute you with tears.
And, coming out on the green from *The Parting Pot,*
I notice a bicycle-tyre
Hanging from the high stone feathers of your
    monument.

England, 20th century

My body in the walls captived

Sir Walter Ralegh

My body in the walls captived
Feels not the wound of spiteful envy
But my thralled mind, of liberty deprived,
Fast fettered in her ancient memory,
Doth nought behold but sorrow's dying face,
Such prison erst was so delightful
As it desired no other dwelling place;
But time's effects and destinies despiteful
Have changed both my keeper and my fare;
Love's fire and beauty's light I then had store,
But now close kept, as captives wonted are:
That food, that heat, that light I find no more;
Despair bolts up my doors, and I alone
Speak to dead walls, but those hear not my moan.

England, 16th century

from Samson Agonistes

John Milton

Messenger: Occasions drew me early to this city;
 And, as the gates I entered with sun-rise,
 The morning trumpets festival proclaimed
 Through each high street. Little I had dispatched,
 When all abroad was rumoured that this day
 Samson should be brought forth, to show the people
 Proof of his mighty strength in feats and games.
 I sorrowed at his captive state, but minded
 Not to be absent at that spectacle.
 The building was a spacious theatre,
 Half round on two main pillars vaulted high,
 With seats where all the lords, and each degree
 Of sort, might sit in order to behold;
 The other side was open, where the throng,
 On banks and scaffolds under sky might stand.
 I among these aloof obscurely stood.
 The feast and noon grew high, and sacrifice
 Had filled their hearts with mirth, high cheer, and wine,
 When to their sports they turned. Immediately
 Was Samson as a public servant brought,
 In their state livery clad: before him pipes
 And timbrels; on each side went armed guards;
 Both horse and foot before him and behind,
 Archers and slingers, cataphracts, and spears.
 At sight of him the people with a shout
 Rifted the air, clamouring their god with praise,
 Who had made their dreadful enemy their thrall.
 He patient, but undaunted, where they led him,
 Came to the place; and what was set before him,
 Which without help of eye might be assayed,
 To heave, pull, draw, or break, he still performed
 All with incredible, stupendious force,
 None daring to appear antagonist.

At length, for intermission sake, they led him
Between the pillars; he his guide requested
(For so from such as nearer stood we heard),
As over-tired, to let him lean a while
With both his arms on those two massy pillars,
That to the arched roof gave main support.
He unsuspicious led him; which when Samson
Felt in his arms, with head a while inclined,
And eyes fast fixed, he stood, as one who prayed,
Or some great matter in his mind revolved:
At last, with head erect, thus cried aloud:—
'Hitherto, Lords, what your commands imposed
I have performed, as reason was, obeying,
Not without wonder or delight beheld;
Now, of my own accord, such other trial
I mean to show you of my strength yet greater
As with amaze shall strike all who behold.'
This uttered, straining all his nerves, he bowed;
As with the force of winds and waters pent
When mountains tremble, those two massy pillars
With horrible convulsion to and fro
He tugged, he shook, till down they came, and drew
The whole roof after them with burst of thunder
Upon the heads of all who sat beneath,
Lords, ladies, captains, counsellors, or priests,
Their choice nobility and flower, not only
Of this, but each Philistian city round,
Met from all parts to solemnize this feast.
Samson, with these immixed, inevitably
Pulled down the same destruction on himself;
The vulgar only scaped, who stood without.

England, 17th century

Holy Sonnet VII

John Donne

At the round earth's imagined corners, blow
Your trumpets, Angels, and arise, arise
From death, you numberless infinities
Of souls, and to your scattered bodies go,
All whom the flood did, and. fire shall o'erthrow,
All whom war, dearth, age, agues, tyrannies,
Despair, law, chance, hath slain, and you whose eyes,
Shall behold God, and never taste death's woe.
But let them sleep, Lord, and me mourn a space,
For, if above all these, my sins abound,
'Tis late to ask abundance of thy grace,
When we are there; here on this lowly ground,
Teach me how to repent; for that's as good
As if thou hadst sealed my pardon, with thy blood.

England, 17th century

from Holy Sonnet V

John Donne

I am a little world made cunningly
Of elements, and an angelic spright . . .

England, 17th century

175

A slumber did my spirit seal

William Wordsworth

A slumber did my spirit seal;
  I had no human fears:
She seemed a thing that could not feel
  The touch of earthly years.

No motion has she now, no force;
  She neither hears nor sees;
Rolled round in earth's diurnal course,
  With rocks, and stones, and trees.

England, 19th century

Postscript

W. H. Auden

Since he weighs nothing,
Even the stoutest dreamer
Can fly without wings.

U.S.A., 20th century

Lights Out

Edward Thomas

I have come to the borders of sleep,
The unfathomable deep
Forest where all must lose
Their way, however straight,
Or winding, soon or late;
They cannot choose.

Many a road and track
That, since the dawn's first crack,
Up to the forest brink,
Deceived the travellers,
Suddenly now blurs,
And in they sink.

Here love ends,
Despair, ambition ends;
All pleasure and all trouble,
Although most sweet or bitter,
Here ends in sleep that is sweeter
Than tasks most noble.

There is not any book
Or face of dearest look
That I would not turn from now
To go into the unknown
I must enter, and leave, alone,
I know not how.

The tall forest towers;
Its cloudy foliage lowers
Ahead, shelf above shelf;
Its silence I hear and obey
That I may lose my way
And myself.

England, 20th century

Sonnet to Sleep

John Keats

O soft embalmer of the still midnight!
　Shutting with careful fingers and benign
Our gloom-pleased eyes, embowered from the light,
　Enshaded in forgetfulness divine;
O soothest sleep! if so it please thee, close,
　In midst of this thine hymn, my willing eyes,
Or wait the amen, ere thy poppy throws
　Around my bed its lulling charities;
　Then save me, or the passèd day will shine
Upon my pillow, breeding many woes;
　Save me from curious conscience, that still lords
Its strength for darkness, burrowing like a mole;
　Turn the key deftly in the oilèd wards,
And seal the hushèd casket of my soul.

England, 19th century

On My Short-Sightedness
Prem Chaya

To my short-sighted eyes,
The world seems better far
Than artificial aid
To sight would warrant it:
The earth is just as green,
The sky a paler blue;
Many a blurred outline
Of overlapping hue;
Shapes, forms are indistinct;
Distance a mystery;
Often a common scene
Conceals a new beauty;
Ugliness is hidden
In a curtain of mist;
And hard, cruel faces
Lose their malignity.
So do not pity me
For my short-sighted eyes;
They see an unknown world
Of wonder and surprise.

Thailand, 20th century

Takahama Kyoshi

In the old man's eyes
The piercing sun
Looks fuddled.

Japan, 20th century
Trans. Bownas & Thwaite

179

Charles

Leonard Clark

He was born blind with the snow on a winter's day;
The moon blank as marble stared at him from the full,
But his mother wept to see the vacant rolling of his eyes;
His father dared not look and despairingly turned away
When hands like feelers fumbled in space to pull
Fingers and lips to upturned face to recognise.
Growing older he sat in the dark learning voices by heart,
Carried on conversations with birds singing in summer trees,
Heard brooks changing their sound at floodtime, the angled
    dart
Of dazzled bats diving through twilight air.
But music played by wandering band or organ at the fair
Moved him to tears and fingers to invisible keys,
So that at twenty-five he began to drown the village
    church
With ceaseless tides of Handel, Bach and Mendelssohn,
And magnified the Lord for seven-and-thirty years.
With egg-shaped head he sat upright upon his perch,
Praying on flute we might depart in peace,
Triumphant came from Egypt on the bombardon,
Made thunderstorms at will, stars race like charioteers,
Captivity to turn, the harvest to increase;
He brought sweet healing to the troubled mind,
Fearlessly opened the eyes of the blind.

England, 20th century

On His Blindness

John Milton

When I consider how my light is spent,
   E're half my days, in this dark world and wide,
   And that one talent which is death to hide,
   Lodged with me useless, though my soul more
      bent
To serve therewith my Maker, and present
   My true account, lest he returning chide:
   Doth God exact day-labour, light denied,
   I fondly ask; but patience, to prevent
That murmur, soon replies, God doth not need
   Either man's work or His own gifts; who best
   Bear His mild yoke, they serve Him best, His state
Is kingly. Thousands at His bidding speed
   And post o'er land and ocean without rest:
   They also serve who only stand and wait.

England, 17th century

Thomas Rymer

Anon.

True Thomas lay on Huntlie bank;
   A ferlie he spied wi' his e'e;
And there he saw a lady bright,
   Come riding down by the Eildon Tree.

Her shirt was o' the grass-green silk,
   Her mantle o' the velvet fine;
At ilka tett of her horse's mane,
   Hung fifty siller bells and nine.

True Thomas, he pulled aff his cap,
   And louted low down to his knee,
'All hail, thou mighty Queen of Heaven!
   For thy peer on earth I never did see.'

'O no, O no, Thomas,' she said;
   'That name does not belang to me;
I am but the Queen of fair Elfland,
   That am hither come to visit thee.

'Harp and carp, Thomas,' she said;
   'Harp and carp along wi' me;
And if ye dare to kiss my lips,
   Sure of your body I will be.'

'Betide me weal, betide me woe,
   That weird shall never danton me.'
Syne he has kissed her rosy lips,
   All underneath the Eildon Tree.

'Now, ye maun go wi' me,' she said;
   'True Thomas, ye maun go wi' me;
And ye maun serve me seven years,
   Through weal or woe as may chance to be.'

She mounted on her milk-white steed;
   She's ta'en true Thomas up behind:
And aye, whene'er her bridle rang,
   The steed flew swifter than the wind.

O they rade on, and farther on;
   The steed gaed swifter than the wind;
Until they reached a desert wide,
   And living land was left behind.

'Light down, light down, now, true Thomas,
    And lean your head upon my knee:
Abide and rest a little space,
    And I will show you ferlies three.

'O see ye not yon narrow road,
    So thick beset with thorns and briars?
That is the path of righteousness,
    Though after it but few enquires.

'And see not ye that braid braid road,
    That lies across that lily leven?
That is the path of wickedness,
    Though some call it the road to heaven.

'And see not ye that bonny road,
    That winds about the fernie brae?
That is the road to fair Elfland,
    Where thou and I this night maun gae.

'But, Thomas, ye maun hold your tongue,
    Whatever ye may hear or see;
For, speak you word in Elfin land,
    Ye'll ne'er go back to your ain country.'

O they rade on, and farther on,
    And they waded through rivers aboon the
            knee,
And they saw neither sun nor moon,
    But they heard the roaring of the sea.

It was mirk mirk night, there was nae stern light,
    They waded through red blude to the knee;
For a' the blude, that's shed on earth,
    Rins through the springs o' that country.

Syne they came on to a garden green,
  And she pu'd an apple frae a tree—
'Take this for thy wages, true Thomas;
  It will give thee the tongue that can never
    lie.'

'My tongue is mine ain,' true Thomas said;
  'A gudely gift ye wad gie to me!
I neither dought to buy nor sell,
  At fair or tryst where I may be.

'I dought neither speak to prince or peer,
  Nor ask of grace from fair lady.'
'Now hold thy peace!' the lady said,
  'For as I say, so must it be.'

He has gotten a coat of the even cloth,
  And a pair of shoes of velvet green;
And, till seven years were gane and past,
  True Thomas on earth was never seen.

Scotland, trad.

from Fifteen Poems of My Heart

Juan Chi

Once I dressed up
To receive a guest
Who was strange to me
And airy like a grain of flying dust.
Clouds trailed after his robes.
His subtle words were pearls,
So short a time did he remain.
When shall I meet him again?

China, 3rd century
Trans. Ch'ên & Bullock

The King of China's Daughter

Edith Sitwell

The King of China's daughter,
She never would love me
Though I hung my cap and bells upon
Her nutmeg tree.
For oranges and lemons,
The stars in bright blue air
(I stole them long ago my dear),
Were dangling there.
The Moon did give me silver pence,
The Sun did give me gold,
And both together softly blew
And made my porridge cold;
But the King of China's daughter
Pretended not to see
When I hung my cap and bells upon
Her nutmeg tree.

The King of China's daughter,
So beautiful to see
With her face like yellow water
Left her nutmeg tree.
Her little rope for skipping
She kissed and gave it me
Made of painted notes of singing birds
Among the fields of tea.
I skipped across the nutmeg field
I skipped across the sea
And neither sun nor moon my dear
Has yet caught me.

England, 20th century

from Romeo and Juliet

William Shakespeare

O, then, I see Queen Mab hath been with you.
She is the fairies' midwife; and she comes
In shape no bigger than an agate-stone
On the fore-finger of an alderman,
Drawn with a team of little atomies
Athwart men's noses as they lie asleep:
Her waggon-spokes made of long spinners' legs,
The cover, of the wings of grass hoppers;
Her traces, of the smallest spider's web;
Her collars, of the moonshine's watery beams;
Her whip, of cricket's bone; the lash, of film;
Her waggoner, a small grey-coated gnat,
Not half so big as a round little worm
Pricked from the lazy finger of a maid:
Her chariot is an empty hazel-nut,
Made by the joiner squirrel or old grub,
Time out o'mind the fairies' coachmakers.
And in this state she gallops night by night
Through lovers' brains, and then they dream of love:
O'er courtiers' knees, that dream on court'sies
        straight;
O'er lawyers' fingers, who straight dream on fees:
O'er ladies' lips, who straight on kisses dream,
Which oft the angry Mab with blisters plagues,
Because their breaths with sweatmeats tainted are:
Sometime she gallops o'er a courtier's nose,
And then dreams he of smelling out a suit:
And sometime comes she with a tithe-pig's tail,
Tickling a parson's nose as a' lies asleep,
Then dreams he of another benefice:
Sometime she driveth o'er a soldier's neck,
And then dreams he of cutting foreign throats,
Of breaches, ambuscadoes, Spanish blades,

Of healths five fathoms deep; and then anon
Drums in his ear, at which he starts and wakes,
And being thus frighted, swears a prayer or two,
And sleeps again. This is that very Mab
That plaits the manes of horses in the night,
And bakes the elf-locks in foul sluttish hairs,
Which, once untangled, much misfortune bodes:
This is the hag, when maids lie on their backs,
That presses them, and learns them first to bear,
Making them women of good carriage:
This is she—

England, 16th century

from The Tempest

William Shakespeare

Be not afeared; the isle is full of noises,
Sounds and sweet airs, that give delight, and
    hurt not.
Sometimes a thousand twanging instruments
Will hum about mine ears; and sometimes voices,
That, if I then had waked after long sleep,
Will make me sleep again: and then, in dreaming,
The clouds methought would open, and show riches
Ready to drop upon me; that, when I waked,
I cried to dream again.

England, 16th century

Merlin

Edwin Muir

O Merlin in your crystal cave
Deep in the diamond of the day,
Will there ever be a singer
Whose music will smooth away
The furrow drawn by Adam's finger
Across the meadow and the wave?
Or a runner who'll outrun
Man's long shadow driving on,
Break through the gate of memory
And hang the apple on the tree?
Will your magic ever show
The sleeping bride shut in her bower,
The day wreathed in its mound of snow
And Time locked in his tower?

England, 20th century

from The Land of Heart's Desire

W. B. Yeats

The wind blows out of the gates of the day,
The wind blows over the lonely of heart,
And the lonely of heart is withered away;
While the faeries dance in a place apart,
Shaking their milk-white feet in a ring,
Tossing their milk-white arms in the air;
For they hear the wind laugh and murmur and sing
Of a land where even the old are fair,
And even the wise are merry of tongue;
But I heard a reed of Coolaney say—
'When the wind has laughed and murmured and
    sung,
The lonely of heart is withered away.'

Ireland, 20th century

from The Sleeping Beauty

Edith Sitwell

The fairies all received an invitation,
Ordered their sedan-chairs with great elation,

Their richest trains, their plumes, and their bright trumps
Like silver fruits that from dark branches grow in clumps.

The fays descend from each dark palanquin
With fanfares and with lute sounds, walk within

The shade; there, smiling dim as satyr-broods
Hornèd as moons, that haunt our deepest woods,

Are country gentlemen, so countrified
That in their rustic grace they try to hide

Their fingers sprouting into leaves; we see
Them sweet as cherries growing from a tree—

All fire and snow; they grow and never move,
Each in the grace of his Pan-haunted grove.

'Her mouth,' the first fay said, 'as fair shall be
As any gentle ripe red strawberry

That grows among the thickest silver leaves;
Her locks shall be as blond as these—the eve's

Great winds of beauty, fleeces from those flocks
That Dian tends in her deep woods, those locks

Shall seem.' The second fairy said,
'Blessings like dew fall on her lovely head!

For lovely as the cherubim's soft breath
Or Leda's love, whose cold melodious death

Is heavenly music to the sad world lost,
Her skin shall be, as fair as silver frost.'

But now within the dark shade of a deep-dreaming tree
A darker shade and panoply we see;

Drowning the soft sound of the plashing lute
A great fanfare is heard, like unripe silver fruit.

'Who is this now who comes?' Dark words reply and
            swoon
Through all the high cold arbours of the moon:

'The slighted Laidronette, the unbidden fay,
Princess of the Pagodas . . . Shades, make way!'

The sedan-chair that hides her shade is mellow
As the trees' great fruit-jewels glittering yellow,

And round it the old turbaned ladies flock
Like apes that try to pluck an apricock.

The little fawning airs are trembling wan;
And silver as fair Leda's love the swan,

The moonlight seems; the apricocks have turned to amber,
Cold as from the bright nymph Thetis' chamber,

And far away, the fountains sigh forlorn
As waving rustling sheaves of silver corn.

The wicked fay descended, mopping, mowing
In her wide-hooped petticoat, her water-flowing

Brightly-perfumed silks. . . . 'Ah, ha, I see
You have remembered all the fays but me!'

(She whipped her panthers, golden as the shade
Of afternoon in some deep forest glade.)

'I am very cross because I am old,
And my tales are told
And my flames jewel-cold.

I will make your bright birds scream,
I will darken your jewelled dream,
I will spoil your thickest cream.

I will turn the cream sour,
I will darken the bower,
I will look through the darkest shadows and lour—

And sleep as dark as the shade of a tree
Shall cover you. . . . Don't answer me!
For if the Princess prick her finger
Upon a spindle, then she shall be lost
As a child wandering in a glade of thorn,
With sleep like roses blowing soft, forlorn,
Upon each bough. This, madam, is the cost
Of your dark rudeness. But I will not linger.'

And with a dark dream's pomp and panoply
She swept out with her train; the soft sounds die
Of plumaged revelry bright as her train
Of courtiers; and all was night again.

England, 20th century

Legend

Judith Wright

The blacksmith's boy went out with a rifle
and a black dog running behind.
Cobwebs snatched at his feet,
rivers hindered him,
thorn branches caught at his eyes to make him blind
and the sky turned into an unlucky opal,
but he didn't mind,
I can break branches, I can swim rivers, I can stare out
    any spider I meet,
said he to his dog and his rifle.

The blacksmith's boy went over the paddocks
with his old black hat on his head.
Mountains jumped in his way,
rocks rolled down on him,
and the old crow cried, You'll soon be dead.
And the rain came down like mattocks.
But he only said
I can climb mountains, I can dodge rocks, I can shoot
    an old crow any day,
and he went on over the paddocks.

When he came to the end of the day the sun began falling.
Up came the night ready to swallow him,
like the barrel of a gun,
like an old black hat,
like a black dog hungry to follow him.
Then the pigeon, the magpie and the dove began wailing
and the grass lay down to billow him.
His rifle broke, his hat flew away and his dog was gone
and the sun was falling.

But in front of the night the rainbow stood on a mountain,
just as his heart foretold.
He ran like a hare,
he climbed like a fox;
he caught it in his hands, the colour and the cold—
like a bar of ice, like the column of a fountain,
like a ring of gold.
The pigeon, the magpie and the dove flew up to stare,
and the grass stood up again on the mountain.

The blacksmith's boy hung the rainbow on his shoulder
instead of his broken gun.
Lizards ran out to see,
snakes made way for him,
and the rainbow shone as brightly as the sun.
All the world said, Nobody is braver, nobody is bolder,
nobody else has done
anything to equal it. He went home as bold as he could be
with the swinging rainbow on his shoulder.

Australia, 20th century

Autobiography

Louis MacNeice

In my childhood trees were green
And there was plenty to be seen.

Come back early or never come.

My father made the walls resound,
He wore his collar the wrong way round.

Come back early or never come.

My mother wore a yellow dress;
Gently, gently, gentleness.

Come back early or never come.

When I was five the black dreams came;
Nothing after was quite the same.

Come back early or never come.

The dark was talking to the dead;
The lamp was dark beside my bed.

Come back early or never come.

When I woke they did not care;
Nobody, nobody was there.

Come back early or never come.

When my silent terror cried,
Nobody, nobody replied.

Come back early or never come.

I got up; the chilly sun
Saw me walk away alone.

Come back early or never come.

Ireland, 20th century

Warning to Children

Robert Graves

Children, if you dare to think
Of the greatness, rareness, muchness,
Fewness of this precious only
Endless world in which you say
You live, you think of things like this:
Blocks of slate enclosing dappled
Red and green, enclosing tawny
Yellow nets, enclosing white
And black acres of dominoes,
Where a neat brown paper parcel
Tempts you to untie the string.
In the parcel a small island,
On the island a large tree,
On the tree a husky fruit.
Strip the husk and pare the rind off:
In the kernel you will see
Blocks of slate enclosed by dappled
Red and green, enclosed by tawny
Yellow nets, enclosed by white
And black acres of dominoes,
Where the same brown paper parcel—
Children, leave the string alone!
For who dares undo the parcel
Finds himself at once inside it,
On the island, in the fruit,
Blocks of slate about his head,
Finds himself enclosed by dappled
Green and red, enclosed by yellow
Tawny nets, enclosed by black
And white acres of dominoes,
With the same brown paper parcel
Still unopened on his knee.

And, if he then should dare to think
Of the fewness, muchness, rareness,
Greatness of this endless only
Precious world in which he says
He lives—he then unties the string.

England, 20th century

Lollocks

Robert Graves

By sloth on sorrow fathered,
These dusty-featured Lollocks
Have their nativity in all disordered
Backs of cupboard drawers.

They play hide and seek
Among collars and novels
And empty medicine bottles,
And letters from abroad
That never will be answered.

Every sultry night
They plague little children,
Gurgling from the cistern,
Humming from the air,
Skewing up the bed-clothes,
Twitching the blind.

When the imbecile agèd
Are over-long in dying
And the nurse drowses,
Lollocks come skipping
Up the tattered stairs
And are nasty together
In the bed's shadow.

The signs of their presence
Are boils on the neck,
Dreams of vexation suddenly recalled
In the middle of the morning,
Languor after food.

Men cannot see them,
Men cannot hear them,
Do not believe in them—
But suffer the more
Both in neck and belly.

Women can see them—
O those naughty wives
Who sit by the fireside
Munching bread and honey,
Watching them in mischief
From corners of their eyes,
Slily allowing them to lick
Honey-sticky fingers.

Sovereign against Lollocks
Are hard broom and soft broom,
To well comb the hair,
To well brush the shoe,
And to pay every debt
As it falls due.

England, 20th century

The Collier

Vernon Watkins

When I was born on Amman hill
A dark bird crossed the sun.
Sharp on the floor the shadow fell,
I was the youngest son.

197

And when I went to the County School
I worked in a shaft of light.
In the wood of the desk I cut my name:
Dai for Dynamite.

The tall black hills my brothers stood;
Their lessons all were done.
From the door of the school when I ran out
They frowned to watch me run.

The slow grey bells they rung a chime
Surly with grief or age.
Clever or clumsy, lad or lout,
All would look for a wage.

I learned the valley flowers' names
And the rough bark knew my knees.
I brought home trout from the river
And spotted eggs from the trees.

A coloured coat I was given to wear
Where the lights of the rough land shone.
Still jealous of my favour
The tall black hills looked on.

They dipped my coat in the blood of a kid
And they cast me down a pit,
And although I crossed with strangers
There was no way up from it.

Soon as I went from the County School
I worked in a shaft. Said Jim,
'You will get your chain of gold, my lad,
But not for a likely time.'

And one said, 'Jack was not raised up
When the wind blew out the light
Though he interpreted their dreams
And guessed their fears by night.'

And Tom, he shivered his leper's lamp
For the stain that round him grew;
And I heard mouths pray in the after-damp
When the picks would not break through.

They changed words there in the darkness
And still through my head they run,
And white on my limbs is the linen sheet
And gold on my neck the sun.

Wales, 20th century

The Daemon Lover

Anon.

'O where have you been, my long, long love,
    This seven long years and more?'
'O I'm come to seek my former vows
    Ye granted me before.'

'O hold your tongue of your former vows,
    For they will breed sad strife;
O hold your tongue of your former vows,
    For I am become a wife.'

He turned him right and round about,
    And the tear blinded his ee:
'I wad never hae trodden on Irish ground,
    If it had not been for thee.

'I might have had a king's daughter,
   Far, far beyond the sea;
I might have had a king's daughter,
   Had it not been for love o' thee.'

'If ye might have had a king's daughter,
   Yersel ye had to blame;
Ye might have taken the king's daughter,
   For ye kend that I was nane....

'If I was to leave my husband dear,
   And my two babes also,
O what have you to take me to,
   If with you I should go?'

'I hae seven ships upon the sea—
   The eighth brought me to land—
With four-and-twenty bold mariners,
   And music on every hand.'

She has taken up her two little babes,
   Kissed them baith cheek and chin:
'O fair ye weel, my ain two babes,
   For I'll never see you again.'

She set her foot upon the ship,
   No mariners could she behold;
But the sails were o' the taffetie,
   And the masts o' the beaten gold.

She had not sailed a league, a league,
   A league but barely three,
When dismal grew his countenance,
   And drumlie grew his ee....

They had not sailed a league, a league,
    A league but barely three,
Until she espied his cloven foot,
    And she wept right bitterly.

'O hold your tongue of your weeping,' says he,
    'Of your weeping now let me be:
I will shew you how the lilies grow
    On the banks of Italy.'

'O what hills are yon, yon pleasant hills,
    That the sun shines sweetly on?'
'O yon are the hills of heaven,' he said,
    'Where you will never win.'

'O whaten a mountain is yon,' she said,
    'All so dreary wi' frost and snow?'
'O yon is the mountain of hell,' he cried,
    'Where you and I will go.' . . .

He strack the tap-mast wi' his hand,
    The fore-mast wi' his knee,
And he brake that gallant ship in twain,
    And sank her in the sea.

Scotland, trad.

Song

Henry VIII

As the holly groweth green,
    And never changeth hue,
So I am, ever hath been,
    Unto my lady true;

As the holly groweth green
    With ivy all alone,
When flowerës can not be seen
    And greenwood leaves be gone.

Now unto my lady
    Promise to her I make,
From all other only
    To her I me betake.

Adieu, mine own lady,
    Adieu, my special,
Who hath my heart truly
    Be sure, and ever shall!

England, 16th century

The Maidens Came

Anon.

The maidens came
When I was in my mother's bower
I had all that I would.
The baily beareth the bell away
The lily, the rose, the rose I lay,
The silver is white, red is the gold;
The robes they lay in fold;
The baily beareth the bell away
The lily, the rose, the rose I lay;
And through the glass window
Shines the sun.
How should I love and I so young?
The baily beareth the bell away,
The lily, the rose, the rose I lay.

England, 15th century

All in green went my love riding
on a great horse of gold
into the silver dawn.

four lean hounds crouched low and smiling
the merry deer ran before.

Fleeter be they than dappled dreams
the swift sweet deer
the red rare deer.

Four red roebuck at a white water
the cruel bugle sang before.

Horn at hip went my love riding
riding the echo down
into the silver dawn.

four lean hounds crouched low and smiling
the level meadows ran before.

Softer be they than slippered sleep
the lean lithe deer
the fleet flown deer.

Four fleet does at a gold valley
the famished arrow sang before.

Bow at belt went my love riding
riding the mountain down
into the silver dawn.

four lean hounds crouched low and smiling
the sheer peaks ran before.

Paler be they than daunting death
the sleek slim deer
the tall tense deer.

Four tall stags at a green mountain
the lucky hunter sang before.

All in green went my love riding
on a great horse of gold
into the silver dawn.

four lean hounds crouched low and smiling
my heart fell dead before.

U.S.A., 20th century

from Lamia

John Keats

She was a gordian shape of dazzling hue,
Vermilion-spotted, golden, green, and blue;
Striped like a zebra, freckled like a pard,
Eyed like a peacock, and all crimson-barred;
And full of silver moons, that, as she breathed,
Dissolved, or brighter shone, or interwreathed
Their lustres with the gloomier tapestries—
So rainbow-sided, touched with miseries,
She seemed at once, some penanced lady elf,
Some demon's mistress, or the demon's self.
Upon her crest she wore a wannish fire
Sprinkled with stars, like Ariadne's tiar:
Her head was serpent, but ah, bitter-sweet!
She had a woman's mouth with all its pearls complete;
And for her eyes: what could such eyes do there
But weep, and weep, that they were born so fair?
As Proserpine still weeps for her Sicilian air.

England, 19th century

Kobayashi Issa

Stop! don't swat the fly
Who wrings his hands,
Who wrings his feet.

Japan, 19th century
Trans. Bownas & Thwaite

The Silkworms

Douglas Stewart

All their lives in a box! What generations,
What centuries of masters, not meaning to be cruel
But needing their labour, taught these creatures such patience
That now though sunlight strikes on the eye's dark jewel
Or moonlight breathes on the wing they do not stir
But like the ghosts of moths crouch silent there.

Look, it's a child's toy! There is no lid even,
They can climb, they can fly, and all the world's their tree;
But hush, they say in themselves, we are in prison.
There is no word to tell them that they are free,
And they are not; ancestral voices bind them
In dream too deep for wind or word to find them.

Even in the young, each like a little dragon
Ramping and green upon his mulberry leaf,
So full of life, it seems, the voice has spoken:
They hide where there is food, where they are safe,
And the voice whispers, 'Spin the cocoon,
Sleep, sleep, you shall be wrapped in me soon.'

Now is their hour, when they wake from that long swoon;
Their pale curved wings are marked in a pattern of leaves,
Shadowy for trees, white for the dance of the moon;
And when on summer nights the buddleia gives
Its nectar like lilac wine for insects mating
They drink its fragrance and shiver, impatient with waiting,

They stir, they think they will go. Then they remember
It was forbidden, forbidden, ever to go out;
The Hands are on guard outside like claps of thunder,
The ancestral voice says Don't, and they do not.
Still the night calls them to unimaginable bliss
But there is terror around them, the vast, the abyss,

And here is the tribe that they know, in their known place,
They are gentle and kind together, they are safe for ever,
And all shall be answered at last when they embrace.
White moth moves closer to moth, lover to lover.
There is that pang of joy on the edge of dying—
Their soft wings whirr, they dream that they are flying.

Australia, 20th century

Chisoku

The face of the dragonfly
Is practically nothing
But eyes.

Japan, 17th century
Trans. R. H. Blyth

Mosquito

John Updike

On the fine wire of her whine she walked,
Unseen in the ominous bedroom dark.
A traitor to her camouflage, she talked
A thirsty blue streak distinct as a spark.

I was to her a fragrant lake of blood
From which she had to sip a drop or die.
A reservoir, a lavish field of food,
I lay awake, unconscious of my size.

We seemed fair-matched opponents. Soft she dropped
Down like an anchor on her thread of song.
Her nose sank thankfully in; then I slapped
At the sting on my arm, cunning and strong.

A cunning, strong Gargantua, I struck
This lover pinned in the feast of my flesh,
Lulled by my blood, relaxed, half-sated, stuck
Engrossed in the gross rivers of myself.

Success! Without a cry the creature died,
Became a fleck of fluff upon the sheet.
The small welt of remorse subsides as side
By side we, murderer and murdered, sleep.

U.S.A., 20th century

Precision

Peter Collenette

A small red-painted helicopter
buzzes straight and undeviating
overhead.
Rotors clatter,
turning smoothly in pivots of oiled steel.
Bolts, springs, blades, plates,
cool,
efficient,
combine smoothly
and move.
It is guided by man:
this is man's precision.

A small red carrot-fly
(the colour is built-in)
whirrs along an indefinite flight path.

Its wings are finely stressed
to the height
of strength and flexibility.
Its built-in guidance system—
a superbly miniaturised computer—
is effectively served
by a wide-angle video-scanner
and twin, highly sensitive antennae.
These combine
to form
an internally guided,
highly manoeuvrable
living flying machine.
God forms it to guide itself;
this is God's precision.

England, 20th century

Flying Crooked

Robert Graves

The butterfly, a cabbage-white,
(His honest idiocy of flight)
Will never now, it is too late,
Master the art of flying straight,
Yet has—who knows so well as I?—
A just sense of how not to fly:
He lurches here and here by guess
And God and hope and hopelessness.
Even the aerobatic swift
Has not his flying-crooked gift.

England, 20th century

The Bat

Theodore Roethke

By day the bat is cousin to the mouse.
He likes the attic of an aging house.

His fingers make a hat about his head.
His pulse beat is so low we think him dead.

He loops in crazy figures half the night
Among the trees that face the corner light.

But when he brushes up against a screen,
We are afraid of what our eyes have seen:

For something is amiss or out of place
When mice with wings can wear a human face.

U.S.A., 20th century

The Worm
from The Book of Thel

William Blake

'Thou seest me the meanest thing, and so I am indeed.
'My bosom of itself is cold, and of itself is dark;
'But he, that loves the lowly, pours his oil upon my head,
'And kisses me, and binds his nuptial bands around my breast,
'And says: "Thou mother of my children, I have loved thee
' "And I have given thee a crown that none can take away." '

England, 19th century

Takahama Kyoshi

The snake fled,
But the eyes that watched
Still in the grass.

Japan, 20th century
Trans. Bownas & Thwaite

Emily Dickinson

A narrow fellow in the grass
Occasionally rides;
You may have met him,—did you not?
His notice sudden is.

The grass divides as with a comb,
A spotted shaft is seen;
And then it closes at your feet
And opens further on.

He likes a boggy acre,
A floor too cool for corn.
Yet when a boy, and barefoot,
I more than once, at noon,

Have passed, I thought, a whip-lash
Unbraiding in the sun,—
When, stooping to secure it,
It wrinkled, and was gone.

Several of nature's people
I know, and they know me;
I feel for them a transport
Of cordiality;

But never met this fellow,
Attended or alone,
Without a tighter breathing,
And zero at the bone.

U.S.A., 19th century

Considering the Snail

Thom Gunn

The snail pushes through a green
night, for the grass is heavy
with water and meets over
the bright path he makes, where rain
has darkened the earth's dark. He
moves in a wood of desire,

pale antlers barely stirring
as he hunts. I cannot tell
what power is at work, drenched there
with purpose, knowing nothing.
What is a snail's fury? All
I think is that if later

I parted the blades above
the tunnel and saw the thin
trail of broken white across
litter, I would never have
imagined the slow passion
to that deliberate progress.

England, 20th century

The Odyssey of a Snail

Federico García Lorca

Now over the path
An undulating silence
Flows from the olive grove.
With a group of red ants
He next encounters.
They are going along angrily,
And dragging behind them
Another ant with his
Antennae clipped off.

The snail exclaims:
'Little ants, have patience.
Why do you thus illtreat
Your companion?
Tell me what he has done,
And I will judge in good faith;
Relate it, little ant.'
The ant, by now half-dead,
Says very sadly,
'I have seen the stars.'
'What are stars?' say
The other ants uneasily.
And the snail asks
Pensively, 'The stars?'
The ant repeats,
'I have seen the stars.
I went up to the highest tree
In the whole poplar grove,
And saw thousands of eyes
In my own darkness.'
The snail asks again,
'But what are stars?'
'They are lights which we carry
On the top of our heads.'
'We do not see them,'
The other ants remark.
And the snail says 'My eyesight
Only reaches to the grass.'
The ants exclaim,
Waving their antennae,
'We shall kill you
You are lazy and perverse;
To labour is your law.'
'I have seen the stars,'
Says the wounded ant.
And the snail passes judgement:

'Let him go free,
Continue your work.
It's likely that soon,
Worn out, he will perish.'

Across the mild wind
A bee has passed.
The agonising ant
Inhales the vast evening
And says, 'It is she who comes
To take me to a star.'

The other ants run off
On seeing he has died.

The snail sighs
And goes off amazed
And full of confusion
At the eternal. 'The path
Has no end,' he exclaims . . .

Spain, 20th century
Trans. Roy Campbell

Kobayashi Issa

Red sky in the morning:
Does it gladden you,
O snail?

Japan, 19th century
Trans. Bownas & Thwaite

Kobayashi Issa

Where can he be going
In the rain
This snail?

Japan, 19th century
Trans. R. H. Blyth

Kangaroo

D. H. Lawrence

In the northern hemisphere
Life seems to leap at the air, or skim under the wind
Like stags on rocky ground, or pawing horses, or
    springy scut-tailed rabbits.

Or else rush horizontal to charge at the sky's horizon,
Like bulls or bisons or wild pigs.

Or slip like water slippery towards its ends,
As foxes, stoats, and wolves, and prairie dogs.

Only mice, and moles, and rats, and badgers, and
    beavers, and perhaps bears
Seem belly-plumbed to the earth's mid-navel.
Or frogs that when they leap come flop, and flop to
    the centre of the earth.

But the yellow antipodal Kangaroo, when she sits up,
Who can unseat her, like a liquid drop that is heavy,
    and just touches earth.

The downward drip
The down-urge.
So much denser than cold-blooded frogs.

Delicate mother Kangaroo
Sitting up there rabbit-wise, but huge, plump-
    weighted,
And lifting her beautiful slender face, oh! so much
    more gently and finely lined than a rabbit's, or
    than a hare's,
Lifting her face to nibble at a round white peppermint
    drop which she loves, sensitive mother Kangaroo.

Her sensitive, long, pure-bred face.
Her full antipodal eyes, so dark,
So big and quiet and remote, having watched so
    many empty dawns in silent Australia.

Her little loose hands, and drooping Victorian
    shoulders.
And then her great weight below the waist, her vast
    pale belly
With a thin young yellow little paw hanging out,
    and straggle of a long thin ear, like ribbon,
Like a funny trimming to the middle of her belly,
    thin little dangle of an immature paw, and one
    thin ear.

Her belly, her big haunches
And, in addition, the great muscular python-stretch
    of her tail.

There, she shan't have any more peppermint drops.
So she wistfully, sensitively sniffs the air, and then
    turns, goes off in slow sad leaps

On the long flat skis of her legs,
Steered and propelled by that steel-strong snake of a
    tail.
Stops again, half turns, inquisitive to look back.
While something stirs quickly in her belly, and a lean
    little face comes out, as from a window,
Peaked and a bit dismayed,
Only to disappear again quickly away from the sight
    of the world, to snuggle down in the warmth,
Leaving the trail of a different paw hanging out.

Still she watches with eternal, cocked wistfulness!
How full her eyes are, like the full, fathomless,
    shining eyes of an Australian black-boy

Who has been lost so many centuries on the margins
　　　of existence!

She watches with insatiable wistfulness.
Untold centuries of watching for something to come,
For a new signal from life, in that silent lost land of
　　　the South.

Where nothing bites but insects and snakes and the
　　　sun, small life.
Where no bull roared, no cow ever lowed, no stag
　　　cried, no leopard screeched, no lion coughed,
　　　no dog barked,
But all was silent save for parrots occasionally, in the
　　　haunted blue bush.

Wistfully watching, with wonderful liquid eyes.
And all her weight, all her blood, dripping sack-wise
　　　down towards the earth's centre,
And the live little-one taking in its paw at the door
　　　of her belly.

Leap then, and come down on the line that draws to
　　　the earth's deep, heavy centre.

England, 20th century

The Marvellous Bear Shepherd

Anon.

There were two men of holy will
Who lived together without an ill,
All lonely in a hermitage,
As meek as birdës in a cage.
The one was called Eutucylus
The other hight Florentius.

Eutucylus he was the clerk
He taught the people God's work.
Florens he had much less of lore,
But in prayer wrought ever more.
Beside the house an abbey lie
Whereat in time the abbot die.
Then all the monks took them to rede
To choose who should reign in his stede,
And chose for them Eutucylus
To be the abbot of their house.
Upon all hands fell the lot
So Eutucylus was made abbot.
When he was gone Florens gan dwell
Lonely and wistful in his cell;
Withouten brother he made moan
For that he should dwell alone,
And had great sorrow and was dreary
As be they who lose good company.
And prayed he God, that he would have
Some good comfort of His love.
Thus prayed Florens by his bed
That God should send him felauhede.
Thus prayed Florens by his bed
He prayed dear God of him take heed
And rising up and looking out
He saw a bear, wild and stout.
This bear he came unto the gate
He came to where Florens he sate,
And when the bear he came him near
The bear him louted and made fair cheer;
Such fair cheer as a bear might make
And asked meek he would him take.
At this Florens him bethought
That God had heard what he besought
And thanked him of his sweet grace
That he had sent him such solace,

For a miracle he must understand
That a wild bear came so tame to hand.
Now Florens he had six sheep
But no herdsmen them to keep,
So bade the bear that he should go
And drive his sheep to and fro.
'And keep them well that none them tear
And thou shalt be my good bear.'
The bear him louted with semblance glad
For to do what Florens bade,
So to the bear he gave advice:
'Every day when I eat twice
Come thou home at high undurne
And no longer in the field sojourne!
And every day when I fast
At the nones come home at last.'
So did the bear every day,
Nere one hour past he away,
But came he home unto the cell
Always at both times he knew well.
Then Florens had comfort and gain
Of his bear that was so tame,
And loved him much withouten fail
For the miracle and the mervaile;
   And, sooth to say, to him appeared
The bear was a most marvellous herd.
A bear through kind should eat sheep
Yet here as herd he did them keep,
And the miracle might not be hid
The whole country knew it was did
That Florens had a tame bear
That of his sheep the herdsman were.
The Abbot that was Eutucylus
Had four disciples envious
That all day of this bear they spake,
With deep intent evil to make,

And said all four of them between
That it was great evil scorn and mean;
'More mervail did Florentius
Than doth our abbot Eutucylus,'
They said 'that it shall not go so,'
And made forward that bear to slo.
As they said, so evil wrought,
And the dear bear to death they brought.

At evening time the bear came not.
Florens had thereof much thought
He rose and sped him to the field
And after his bear fast beheld
And at last his bear he found,
Beside his sheep, slain, on the ground.

Then had Florens wrath and woe,
To know of evil that was so,
And plained him sore for his own dear
That they had slain his good bear.
Hopeless he plained him wondrous sore,
That his solace was no more.
Of Jesu Christ had they no dread
That they should do this evil deed?
'My gentle bear of good will!
He ne're did no man any ill.
He was sent to me of God's grace,
To be my help and my solace,
That God should send him me for love,
And they'd not suffer him to live.'
Almighty God shall do his will,
On them and all who did this ill.
And above the earth they soon were stinking
That to the bear's death were consenting.

English, medieval

Au Jardin des Plantes

John Wain

The gorilla lay on his back,
One hand cupped under his head,
Like a man.

Like a labouring man tired with work,
A strong man with his strength burnt away
In the toil of earning a living.

Only of course he was not tired out with work,
Merely with boredom; his terrible strength
All burnt away by prodigal idleness.

A thousand days, and then a thousand days,
Idleness licked away his beautiful strength
He having no need to earn a living.

It was all laid on, free of charge,
We maintained him, not for doing anything,
But for being what he was.

And so that Sunday morning he lay on his back
Like a man, like a worn out man,
One hand cupped under his terrible hard head.

Like a man, like a man,
One of those we maintain, not for doing anything,
But for being what they are.

A thousand days, and then a thousand days,
With everything laid on, free of charge,
They cup their heads in prodigal idleness.

England, 20th century

220

The Zoo

Boris Pasternak

The zoo lies in the parkland thickets.
We enter and hold out our tickets
To park attendants who surround
The entrance-arch; and look around.

Here through the gates in grotto fashion
We now encounter in succession
Huge limestone mouldings, and beyond—
The wind-swept silver-surfaced pond,
Throughout peculiarly aquiver,
Seized with an abstract fever-shiver.

Now mixing with haphazard sounds,
The puma's distant roar resounds
All through the park; this far-off roaring
Rolls on like thunder skyward soaring,
Exciting, menacing, and loud—
But there is not a single cloud!

With a good-neighbourly appearance
The children chat with brown-bear parents;
The ringing slabs are damped, one feels,
By thumping bear-cubs' naked heels.

Here, after their exhaustive sunning,
Into their swimming-pool are running
Child, father, mother polar-bear,
In nothing but their underwear.
This trio splashes, roars and pants,
But does not lose the beltless pants,
And no amount of washing betters
The soiled and shaggy trouser-tatters.

221

Prior to dirtying, the vixen
Will look askance and sniff, then fix on
The chosen spot. Avid and lanky,
Their bark like padlocks sharp and clanky,
The wolves are famished in their greed;
Their eyes are full of dried-up heat.
The snapping mother-wolf is stung
By children laughing at her young.

A lioness, the people facing,
Relentlessly the floorboards pacing
And turning on her only track
First there, then back, then there, then back,
Is driven by her very raging
When brushing at the iron caging;
The barrier pattern stark and black,
Is moving with her there and back.

The self same iron pattern sends a
Bewildered panther into frenzy.

The same recurring bars again
Will chase a cheetah on a chain.

More lady-like than any lady
The llama looks when promenading;
She curtseys, spits into your face,
And leaps away with haughty grace.

The desert ship observes with sadness
This shallow act of sudden madness.
The camel's reasoning is wise:
'One does not spit in grown-ups' eyes!'
All round him human waves are surging,
And out of them he is emerging
With his steep rounded camel's breast—
A rowing boat upon a crest.

The garb of guinea-fowl and pheasants
Is brightest Sunday-best of peasants
Here tinsel, steel and silver thread
Are glittering as they are shed.

The peacock: seeing is believing.
A shot-silk shawl of blue-black weaving
He wears, a hot and sooty sight.
He walks, mysterious as night,
Extinguished now behind a turning,
Now once again in splendour burning,
Emerging from behind a fence,
His tail like skies at night immense,
With falling stars defying counting,
Of falling stars a playing fountain.

The parrots push away their trough,
They've had a snack and had enough;
They peck one grain and feel they must
Rub clean their beaks in sheer disgust.
Perhaps because of jokes they crack,
Their tongues like coffee-beans are black.
Some of their family have feathers
Like Persian lilac; some, one gathers,
In error classed as birds, instead
Should blossom on a flower bed.

The scarlet-bottomed great attraction,
The grey baboon is seen in action.
The public seem to like him best.
By quiet lunacy possessed
He either lingers, grinning, baring
His teeth, or suddenly, a daring
Gymnast, into the air he flings
And from the lofty branches swings,
Intent on making an impression.
Or on all fours in poodle fashion

He runs around; or in a twist
Scratches his cheekbone with a fist;
Or else again, as monkeys should,
He pesters you and begs for food.

In a thick-sided tub, decaying,
Lie pickled guts—the notice saying
That this is mud with a reptile:
A young Egyptian crocodile.
He does not look at all aggressive;
When grown he may be more impressive.

By-passing on our way some cages,
Stopping at others, thus in stages
We follow notices which lead
Us 'To The Elephants'. Indeed
Here is the drowsy mass, ascending
Up to the beams, a cartload standing
Within a warehouse, and a flock
Of hay is whirling on the block.
The monster turns around thereafter,
Dislodging block and hay and rafter,
And sweeping up a cloud of husks
Towards the ceiling and the tusks.
His trunk is knitting lofty stitches
Or shuffles over tiles and twitches;
A hoop has made his ankle sore,
He drags a chain along the floor
And something in this dryness hackles:
Perhaps it is the straw that crackles,
Perhaps his ears, patched up and drab,
Like two old aprons of a cab.

Time to return now to the city,
It's getting late, but what a pity!
There are wonders by the score:
We've seen a third perhaps, no more.

For the last time the tramlines' rumbling
Is mingling with an eagle's grumbling,
And street-noise drowns the lions' roar
Just once again and then—no more.

U.S.S.R., 20th century
Trans. Lydia Pasternak

Travelling through the Dark

William Stafford

Travelling through the dark I found a deer
dead on the edge of the Wilson River road.
It is usually best to roll them into the canyon:
that road is narrow; to swerve might make more dead.

By glow of the tail-light I stumbled back of the car
and stood by the heap, a doe, a recent killing;
she had stiffened already, almost cold.
I dragged her off; she was large in the belly.

My fingers touching her side brought me the reason—
her side was warm; her fawn lay there waiting,
alive, still, never to be born.
Beside that mountain road I hesitated.

The car aimed ahead its lowered parking lights;
under the hood purred the steady engine.
I stood in the glare of the warm exhaust turning red;
around our group I could hear the wilderness listen.

I thought hard for us all—my only swerving—
then pushed her over the edge into the river.

U.S.A., 20th century

A Blessing

James Wright

Just off the highway to Rochester, Minnesota,
Twilight bounds softly forth on the grass.
And the eyes of those two Indian ponies
Darken with kindness.
They have come gladly out of the willows
To welcome my friend and me.
We step over the barbed wire into the pasture
Where they have been grazing all day, alone.
They ripple tensely, they can hardly contain their
    happiness
That we have come.
They bow shyly as wet swans. They love each other.
There is no loneliness like theirs.
At home once more,
They begin munching the young tufts of spring in
    the darkness.
I would like to hold the slenderer one in my arms,
For she has walked over to me
And nuzzled my left hand.
She is black and white,
Her mane falls wild on her forehead,
And the light breeze moves me to caress her long ear
That is delicate as the skin over a girl's wrist.
Suddenly I realize
That if I stepped out of my body I would break
Into blossom.

U.S.A., 20th century

226

Fetching Cows
Norman MacCaig

The black one, last as usual, swings her head
And coils a black tongue round a grass tuft. I
Watch her soft weight come down, her split feet spread.

In front, the others swing and slouch; they roll
Their great Greek eyes and breathe out milky gusts
From muzzles black and shiny as wet coal.

The collie trots, bored, at my heels, then plops
Into the ditch. The sea makes a tired sound
That's always stopping though it never stops.

A haycart squats prickeared against the sky.
Hay breath and milk breath. Far out in the West
The wrecked sun founders though its colours fly.

The collie's bored. There's nothing to control . . .
The black cow is two native carriers
Bringing its belly home, slung from a pole.

England, 20th century

Cow
Harold Massingham

Hide of milk-and-honey,
This tense-legged provender
Stands heavier than grand mahogany

Pianos.
      Sculptor, use Cotswold-stone
For such warm secure silence;
Painter, pigment of fawn

For this suede Empress.
         She waits her turn
Insouciant in drizzle tiny as fleas,
Such meaningless self-possession,

A velvet noose round her neck.
Then, slowly as cheesing, psyches turn Indian.
Except the accurate back,

The sacred sensuals have it: swung
Bulge of religious bells,
Blood-and-cream bullion in some swaying

Tub-sided galleon—
But O, her walk, stalwart, a wonder of hundredweights
Borne by sure bone,

Makes mock of a stagger, straight
Past soaking shoulders subdued as by idols:
Until that prim yoking by rosette

Makes her Miss Lancashire of cattle,
Led by a hireling to a gay truck,
Observed by the wet rubies of gloomy bulls.

England, 20th century

The Span of Life

Robert Frost

The old dog barks backward without getting up.
I can remember when he was a pup.

U.S.A., 20th century

Kobayashi Issa

Under the willow
With a leaf stuck in his mouth
The puppy sleeps.

Japan, 19th century
Trans. Lewis Mackenzie

View of a Pig

Ted Hughes

The pig lay on a barrow dead.
It weighed, they said, as much as three men.
Its eyes closed, pink white eyelashes.
Its trotters stuck straight out.

Such weight and thick pink bulk
Set in death seemed not just dead.
It was less than lifeless, further off.
It was like a sack of wheat.

I thumped it without feeling remorse.
One feels guilty insulting the dead,
Walking on graves. But this pig
Did not seem able to accuse.

It was too dead. Just so much
A poundage of lard and pork.
Its last dignity had entirely gone.
It was not a figure of fun.

Too dead now to pity.
To remember its life, din, stronghold
Of earthly pleasure as it had been,
Seemed a false effort, and off the point.

Too deadly factual. Its weight
Oppressed me—how could it be moved?
And the trouble of cutting it up!
The gash in its throat was shocking, but not
    pathetic.

Once I ran at a fair in the noise
To catch a greased piglet
That was faster and nimbler than a cat,
Its squeal was the rending of metal.

Pigs must have hot blood, they feel like ovens.
Their bite is worse than a horse's—
They chop a half-moon clean out.
They eat cinders, dead cats.

Distinctions and admirations such
As this one was long finished with.
I stared at it a long time. They were going to
    scald it,
Scald it and scour it like a doorstep.

England, 20th century

from The Odyssey

THE BOAR HUNT

Homer

When the young Dawn spread in the eastern sky
her finger-tips of rose, the men and dogs
went hunting, taking Odysseus. They climbed
Parnassos' rugged flank mantled in forest,
entering amid high windy folds at noon
when Hêlios beat upon the valley floor
and on the winding Ocean whence he came.
With hounds questing ahead, in open order,
the sons of Autólykos went down a glen,
Odysseus in the lead, behind the dogs,
pointing his long-shadowing spear.
                                        Before them
a great boar lay hid in undergrowth,
in a green thicket proof against the wind
or sun's blaze, fine soever the needling sunlight,
impervious too to any rain, so dense
that cover was, heaped up with fallen leaves.

Patter of hounds' feet, men's feet, woke the boar
as they came up—and from his woody ambush
with razor-back bristling and raging eyes
he trotted and stood at bay. Odysseus,
being on top of him, had the first shot,
lunging to stick him; but the boar
had already charged under the long spear.
He hooked aslant with one white tusk and ripped out
flesh above the knee, but missed the bone.
Odysseus' second thrust went home by luck,
his bright spear passing through the shoulder-joint;
and the beast fell, moaning as life pulsed away.
Autólykos' tall sons took up the wounded,
working skilfully over the Prince Odysseus
to bind his gash, and with a rune they stanched
the dark flow of blood. Then downhill swiftly
they all repaired to the father's house, and there
tended him well—so well they soon could send him,
with Grandfather Autólykos' magnificent gifts,
rejoicing, over sea to Ithaka.

Greece, B.C., date unknown
Trans. Robert Fitzgerald

A Charm against Toothache

John Heath-Stubbs

Venerable Mother Toothache
Climb down from the white battlements,
Stop twisting in your yellow fingers
The fourfold rope of nerves;
And tomorrow I will give you a tot of whisky
To hold in your cupped hands,
A garland of anise-flowers
And three cloves like nails.

231

And tell the attendant gnomes
It is time to knock off now,
To shoulder their little pick-axes,
Their cold-chisels and drills.

And you may mount by a silver ladder
Into the sky, to grind
In the cracked polished mortar
Of the hollow moon
By the lapse of warm waters,
And the poppies nodding like red coals,
The paths on the granite mountains,
And the plantation of my dreams.

England, 20th century

This is Just to Say

William Carlos Williams

I have eaten
the plums
that were in
the icebox

and which
you were probably
saving
for breakfast

Forgive me
they were delicious
so sweet
and so cold

U.S.A., 20th century

Chopsticks

Yüan Mei

I laugh that you should be so busy to pick up morsels,
And put them into others' mouths.
With a lifetime spent amid the sour and the bitter,
Can you or not distinguish the flavours yourself?

China, 18th century
Trans. Kotewıll & Smith

A Charm against the Stitch

Anon.

*Against sudden needle-pains. Feverfew and red-nettle which
grows into a house by a cranny, and dock, boil in butter.*

Loud were they, loud, when they rode in a cloud,
They had but one mind, when they rode in the wind.

Save yourself, that this evil may disappear:
Out, little spear! Out, little spear—
If you're still stuck.

When the Fates ran amuck,
Those mighty old hags on their green-crested nags
Pressing horribly near, and couching their spear,
I stood under cover and darted one over,
An excellent arrow, its aim was so narrow.

Out, little spear,
If you are in!

A smith sat, he forged a forcing-pin,
He hammered the iron, and tempered and tried.

Out, little spear,
If you are inside!

Six smiths forged a bar out clear,
Out, little spear!
Why, you *are* out, spear!

If anything iron's got under thy pelt
The work of a witch, it shall melt, it shall melt!
If you were shot in the skin
Or the flesh or the blood or the limb,
Let it never hurt thee one atom
If it were a shot of a hag or of Satan
Or the shot of an elf, I can fetch
Something useful against an elf; something useful
    against a witch;
Something useful against a devil—I give you my skill!

Flit away by dusk woods to the perilous hill!
Be whole! may God help thee, omnipotent will!

England, c. 10th century
Trans. Gavin Bone

Silent, but . . .

Tsuboi Shigeji

I may be silent, but
I'm thinking.
I may not talk, but
Don't mistake me for a wall.

Japan, 20th century
Trans. Bownas & Thwaite

Alleyway
Salvatore Quasimodo

Sometimes your voices call me back,
and what skies and waters
waken inside me!

A net of sunlight tears
on your walls that at night
were a swaying of lamps
from the late shops
full of wind and sadness.

Other times: a loom thumped in the courtyard,
and at night could be heard a whimper
of puppies and babies.

Alley: a cross of houses
calling out low to each other,
never knowing it is the fear
of being alone in the dark.

Italy, 20th century
Trans. Jack Bevan

from Poems of Solitary Delights
Tachibana Akemi

What a delight it is
When, borrowing
Rare writings from a friend,
I open out
The first sheet.

What delight it is
When, after a hundred days
Of racking my brains,
That verse that wouldn't come
Suddenly turns out well.

What a delight it is
When, of a morning,
I get up and go out
To find in full bloom a flower
That yesterday was not there.

What a delight it is
When I blow away the ash,
To watch the crimson
Of the glowing fire
And hear the water boil.

What a delight it is
When a guest you cannot stand
Arrives, then says to you
'I'm afraid I can't stay long!'
And soon goes home.

What a delight it is
When, skimming through the pages
Of a book, I discover
A man written of there
Who is just like me.

Japan, 19th century
Trans. Bownas & Thwaite

from Paper Boats

Rabindranath Tagore

Day by day I float my paper boats one by one down the
running stream.

In big black letters I write my name on them and the
name of the village where I live.

I hope that someone in some strange land will find
them and know who I am.

I load my little boats with *shiuli* flowers from our
garden, and hope that these blooms of the dawn will be
carried safely to land in the night.

India, 20th century

The Poem of Ten 'Ones'

Hô P'ei Yü

A flower,   Halfway
A willow,   Up the mountain
A fisherman   A priest slowly climbs
On a rock.   To a shrine.

A ray of sun   In the forest
On the river   A yellow leaf
A bird   Flutters and falls.
On the wing.

China, Ch'ing dynasty
Trans. Henry H. Hart

Hints on Pronunciation for Foreigners

T.S.W.

I take it you already know
Of tough and bough and cough and dough?
Others may stumble but not you,
On hiccough, thorough, lough and through?
Well done! And now you wish, perhaps,
To learn of less familiar traps?

Beware of heard, a dreadful word
That looks like beard and sounds like bird,
And dead: it's said like bed, not bead—
For goodness sake don't call it 'deed'!
Watch out for meat and great and threat
(They rhyme with suite and straight and debt.)

A moth is not a moth in mother
Nor both in bother, broth in brother,
And here is not a match for there
Nor dear and fear for bear and pear,
And then there's dose and rose and lose—
Just look them up—and goose and choose,
And cork and work and card and ward,
And font and front and word and sword,
And do and go and thwart and cart—
Come, come, I've hardly made a start!
A dreadful language? Man alive!
I'd mastered it when I was five!

England, 20th century

Arithmetic
Carl Sandburg

Arithmetic is where numbers fly like pigeons in and out of
   your head.
Arithmetic tells you how many you lose or win if you
   know how many you had before you lost or won.
Arithmetic is seven eleven all good children go to heaven
   —or five six bundle of sticks.
Arithmetic is numbers you squeeze from your head to
   your hand to your pencil to your paper till you get the
   answer.
Arithmetic is where the answer is right and everything is
   nice and you can look out of the window and see the
   blue sky—or the answer is wrong and you have to start
   all over and try again and see how it comes out this
   time.

If you take a number and double it and double it again and then double it a few more times, the number gets bigger and bigger and goes higher and higher and only arithmetic can tell you what the number is when you decide to quit doubling.

Arithmetic is where you have to multiply—and you carry the multiplication table in your head and hope you won't lose it.

If you have two animal crackers, one good and one bad, and you eat one and a striped zebra with streaks all over him eats the other, how many animal crackers will you have if somebody offers you five six seven and you say No no no and you say Nay nay nay and you say Nix nix nix?

If you ask your mother for one fried egg for breakfast and she gives you two fried eggs and you eat both of them, who is better in arithmetic, you or your mother?

U.S.A., 20th century

A History Lesson

Miroslav Holub

Kings
like golden gleams
made with a mirror on the wall.

A non-alcoholic pope,
knights without arms,
arms without knights.

The dead like so many strained noodles,
a pound of those fallen in battle,
two ounces of those who were executed,

several heads
like so many potatoes
shaken into a cap—

Geniuses conceived
by the mating of dates
are soaked up by the ceiling into infinity

to the sound of tinny thunder,
the rumble of bellies,
shouts of hurrah,

empires rise and fall
at a wave of the pointer,
the blood is blotted out—

And only one small boy,
who was not paying the least attention,
will ask
between two victorious wars:

And did it hurt in those days too?

Czechoslovakia, 20th century
Trans. George Theiner

The Ruined City

Pao Chao

The immense plain
   runs south to the foamy waves of the sea
   and north to the purple passes of the Great Wall.
In it
   canals are cut through the valleys;
And rivers and roads
   lead to every corner.

In its golden past,
     axles of chariots and carts
     often rubbed against each other
     like men's shoulders.
Shops and houses stood row upon row
And laughter and songs rose up from them.
Glittering and white were the salt fields;
Gloomy and blue were the copper mines.
Wealth and talents
And cavalry and infantry
Reinforced the strict and elaborate
Regulations and laws.
Winding moats and lofty walls
Were dug and built, to ensure
That prosperity would long endure.
People were busy working
On palaces and battlements
And ships and beacon stations
Up and down, far and wide
At all places.
Magnets were installed at mountain passes;
Red lacquer was applied to doors and gates.
The strongholds and fortresses
     would see to it
That for a myriad generations
     the family's rule should last.
But after five centuries or three dynasties
The land was divided like a melon,
Or shared like beans.

Duckweed flourishes in the wells
And brambles block the roads.
Skunks and snakes dwell on sacred altars
While muskdeer and squirrels quarrel on marble steps.
In rain and wind,
Wood elves, mountain ghosts,

Wild rats and foxes
   yawp and scream from dusk to dawn.
Hungry hawks grind their beaks
As cold owls frighten the chicks in their nests.
Tigers and leopards hide and wait
   for a drink of blood
   and a feast of flesh.
Fallen tree-trunks lie lifelessly across
Those once busy highways.
Aspens have long ceased to rustle
And grass dies yellow
In this harsh frosty air
Which grows into a cruelly cold wind.
A solitary reed shakes and twists,
And grains of sand, like startled birds,
   are looking for a safe place to settle.
Bushes and creepers, confused and tangled,
   seem to know no boundaries.

They pull down walls
And fill up moats.
And beyond a thousand miles
Only brown dust flies.
Deep in my thoughts, I sit down and listen
To this awesome silence.

Behind the painted doors and embroidered curtains
There used to be music and dancing.
Hunting or fishing parties were held
In the emerald forests or beside the marble pools.
The melodies from various states
And works of art and rare fish and horses
Are all now dead and buried.
The young girls from east and south
Smooth as silk, fragrant as orchids,

White as jade with their lips red,
Now lie beneath the dreary stones and barren earth.
The greatest displeasure of the largest number
Is the law of nature.
For this ruined city,
I play the lute and sing:
'As the north wind hurries on,
    the battlements freeze.
They tower over the plain
    where there are neither roads nor field-paths.
For a thousand years and a myriad generations,
    I shall watch you to the end in silence.'

China, 5th century
Trans. Ch'ên & Bullock

from The Fire of London

John Dryden

Night came, but without darkness or repose,
    A dismal picture of the general doom:
Where souls distracted when the trumpet blows,
    And half unready with their bodies come.

Those who have homes, when home they do repair,
    To a last lodging call their wandering friends.
Their short uneasy sleeps are broke with care,
    To look how near their own destruction tends.

Those who have none, sit round where once it was,
    And with full eyes each wonted room require:
Haunting the yet warm ashes of the place,
    As murdered men walk where they did expire.

Some stir up coals and watch the vestal fire,
    Others in vain from sight of ruin run:
And, while through burning labyrinths they retire,
    With loathing eyes repeat what they would shun.

The most in fields, like herded beasts lie down;
    To dews obnoxious on the grassy floor:
And while their babes in sleep their sorrows drown,
    Sad parents watch the remnants of their store.

While by the motion of the flames they guess
    What streets are burning now, and what are near:
An infant, waking, to the paps would press,
    And meets, instead of milk, a falling tear.

England, 18th century

Advice to a Knight

T. H. Jones

Wear modest armour; and walk quietly
In woods, where any noise is treacherous.
Avoid dragons and deceptive maidens.

Be polite to other men in armour,
Especially the fierce ones, who are often strong.
Treat all old men as they might be magicians.

So you may come back from your wanderings,
Clink proud and stiff into the queen's court
To doff your helmet and expect her thanks.

The young queen is amused at your white hair,
Asks you to show your notched and rusty sword,
And orders extra straw for your bedding.

Tomorrow put on your oldest clothes,
Take a stout stick and set off again,
It's safer that way if no more rewarding.

Wales, 20th century

from Le Morte Darthur

Thomas Malory

Then the king got his spear in both hands, and ran toward Sir Mordred, crying: Traitor, now is thy death-day come. And when Sir Mordred saw King Arthur, he ran until him with his sword drawn in his hand. And there King Arthur smote Sir Mordred under the shield, with a foin of his spear, throughout the body, more than a fathom. And when Sir Mordred felt that he had his death wound he thrust himself with the might that he had up to the bur of King Arthur's spear. And right so he smote his father Arthur, with his sword holden in both his hands, on the side of the head, that the sword pierced the helmet and the brain-pan, and therewithal Sir Mordred fell stark dead to the earth: and the noble Arthur fell in a swoon to the earth, and there he swooned ofttimes. And Sir Lucan the Butler and Sir Bedivere ofttimes heaved him up. And so weakly betwixt them they led him to a little chapel not far from the sea. And when the king was there he thought him well eased. Then heard they people cry in the field. Now go thou, Sir Lucan, said the king, and do me to wit what betokens that noise in the field. So Sir Lucan departed, for he was grievously wounded in many places. And so as he yede, he saw and hearkened by the moonlight, how that pillers and robbers were come into the field, to pill and to rob many a full noble knight of brooches, and beads, of many a good ring, and many a rich jewel; and who that were not dead all out, they slew them for their harness and their riches. When Sir Lucan understood this work, he came to the king as soon as he might, and told him all what he had heard and seen. Therefore by my rede, said Sir Lucan, it is best that we bring you to some town. I would it were so said the king. But I may not stand my head works so. Ah Sir Launcelot, said King Arthur, this day have I sore missed thee: alas, that ever I was against thee, for now have I my death, whereof Sir Gawaine me warned in my dream. Then Sir Lucan took up the king the one part, and Sir Bedivere the other part, and in the lifting the king swooned; and Sir Lucan fell in a swoon with the lift, that the part of his guts fell out of his body, and there-with the noble knight's heart brast. And when the king awoke, he beheld Sir Lucan, how he lay foaming at the mouth, and part of his guts lay at his feet. Alas, said the king, this is to me a full heavy sight, to see this noble duke so die for my sake, for he would have holpen me, that had more need of help than I. Alas he would not complain him, his heart was so set to help me: now Jesu have mercy upon his soul! Then Sir Bedivere wept for the death of his brother. Leave this mourning and weeping, said the king, for all this will not avail me, for wit thou well an I might live myself, the death of Sir Lucan would grieve me evermore; but my time hieth fast, said the king. Therefore, said Arthur unto Sir Bedivere, take thou Excalibur, my good sword, and go with it to yonder water side, and when thou comest there I charge thee throw my sword in that water, and come again and tell me what thou seest. My lord, said Bedivere, your commandment shall be done, and lightly bring you word again. So Sir Bedivere departed and by the way he beheld that noble sword, that the pommel and the haft was all of precious stones; and then he said to himself: If I throw this rich sword in the water, thereof shall never come good, but harm and loss. And then Sir Bedivere hid Excalibur under a tree. And so, as soon as he might, he came again unto the king, and said he had been at the water, and had thrown the sword in the water. What saw thou there? said the king. Sir, he said, I saw nothing but waves and winds. That is untruly said of thee, said the king, therefore go thou lightly again, and do my commandment; as thou art to me lief and dear, spare not, but throw it in. Then Sir Bevidere returned again, and took the sword in his hand; and then him thought sin and shame to throw away that noble sword, and so eft he hid the sword, and returned again and told to the king that he had been at the water, and done his commandment. What saw thou there? said the king. Sir, he said, I saw nothing but the waters wappe and waves wanne. Ah, traitor untrue, said King Arthur, now hast thou betrayed me twice. Who would have weened that, thou that hast been to me so lief and dear? and thou art named a noble knight, and would betray me for the riches of this sword. But now go again lightly, for thy long tarrying putteth me in great jeopardy of my life, for I have taken cold. And but if thou do now as I bid thee, if ever I may see thee, I shall slay thee with mine own hands; for thou wouldest for my rich sword see me dead. Then Sir Bedivere departed, and went to the sword, and lightly took it up, and went to the water side; and there he bound the girdle about the hilts, and threw the sword as far into the water as he might; and there came an arm and an hand above the water, and met it and caught it, and shook it thrice and brandished, and then vanished with the sword into the water. So Sir Bedivere came again to the king and told him what he saw. Alas said the king, help me hence, for I dread me I have tarried over long. Then Sir Bedivere took the king upon his back, and so went with him to the water side. And when they were there, even fast by the bank hoved a little barge with many fair ladies in it, and among them all was a queen, and all they had black hoods, and all they wept and shrieked when they saw King Arthur. Now put me into the barge, said the king. And so he did softly; and there received him three queens with great mourning; and so they set them down, and in one of their laps King Arthur laid his head. And then that queen said, Ah dear brother, why have ye tarried so long from me? alas, this wound on your head hath caught over-much cold. And anon they rowed from the land, and Sir Bedivere beheld all those ladies go from him. Then Sir Bedivere cried: Ah my lord Arthur, what shall become of me, now ye go from me and leave me here alone among mine enemies? Comfort thyself, said the king, and do as well as thou mayest, for in me is no trust for to trust in; for I must into the Vale of Avilion to heal me of my grievous wound: and if thou hear never more of me, pray for my soul. But ever the queens and ladies wept and shrieked, that it was pity to hear. And as soon as Sir Bedivere had lost the sight of the barge, he wept and wailed, and so took the forest; and so he went all that night, and in the morning he was ware betwixt two holts hoar, of a chapel and an hermitage.

England, 15th century

248

Fighting South of the Ramparts

Anon.

They fought south of the ramparts,
They died north of the wall.
They died in the moors and were not buried
Their flesh was the food of crows.
'Tell the crows we are not afraid;
We have died in the moors and cannot be buried.
Crows, how can our bodies escape you?'
The waters flowed deep
And the rushes in the pool were dark.
The riders fought and were slain;
Their horses wander neighing.
By the bridge there was a house.
Was it south, was it north?
The harvest was never gathered.
How can we give you your offerings?
You served your Prince faithfully,
Though all in vain.
I think of you, faithful soldiers;
Your service shall not be forgotten.
For in the morning you went out to battle
And at night you did not return.

China, c. 1st century
Trans. Arthur Waley

The Parable of the Old Man and the Young
Wilfred Owen

So Abram rose, and clave the wood, and went,
And took the fire with him, and a knife.
And as they sojourned both of them together,
Isaac the first-born spake and said, My Father,
Behold the preparations, fire and iron,
But where the lamb for this burnt-offering?
Then Abram bound the youth with belts and straps,
And builded parapets and trenches there,
And stretchèd forth the knife to slay his son.
When lo! an angel called him out of heaven,
Saying, Lay not thy hand upon the lad,
Neither do anything to him. Behold,
A ram, caught in a thicket by its horns;
Offer the Ram of Pride instead of him.
But the old man would not so, but slew his son,
And half the seed of Europe, one by one.

England, 20th century

Anthem for Doomed Youth
Wilfred Owen

What passing-bells for these who die as cattle?
Only the monstrous anger of the guns.
Only the stuttering rifles' rapid rattle
Can patter out their hasty orisons.
No mockeries now for them; no prayers nor bells,
Nor any voice of mourning save the choirs,—
The shrill, demented choirs of wailing shells;
And bugles calling for them from sad shires.

What candles may be held to speed them all?
Not in the hands of boys, but in their eyes
Shall shine the holy glimmers of good-byes.
The pallor of girls' brows shall be their pall;
Their flowers the tenderness of silent minds,
And each slow dusk a drawing-down of blinds.

England, 20th century

from In Parenthesis (PART 3)

David Jones

So they would go a long while in the solid dark, nor moon, nor battery, dispelled.

Feet plodding in each other's unseen tread. They said no word but to direct their immediate next coming, so close behind to blunder, toe by heel tripping, file-mates; blind on-following, moving with a singular identity.

Half-minds, far away, divergent, own-thought thinking, tucked away unknown thoughts; feet following file friends, each his own thought-maze alone treading; intricate, twist about, own thoughts, all unknown thoughts, to the next so close following on.

He hitched his slipping rifle-sling for the hundredth time over a little where the stretched out surface skin raw rubbed away at his clavicle bone. He thought he might go another half mile perhaps— it must be midnight now of some day of the week. He turned his tired head where the sacking-shield swayed.

Where a white shining waned between its hanging rents, another rises and another; high, unhurrying higher, clear, pale, light-ribbons; very still-bright and bright-showered descent.

Spangled tapestry swayed between the uprights; camouflage-net, meshed with plunging star-draught.

Bobbing night-walkers go against the tossing night-flares.

Intermittent dancing lights betray each salient twist and turn; tiny flickers very low to the south—their meandering world-edge prickt out bright.

Rotary steel hail spit and lashed in sharp spasms along the vibrating line; great solemn guns leisurely manipulated their expensive discharges at rare intervals, bringing weight and full recession to the rising orchestration.

As suddenly the whole world would slip back into a mollifying, untormented dark; their aching bodies knew its calm.

England, 20th century

The Dug-Out

Siegfried Sassoon

Why do you lie with your legs ungainly huddled,
And one arm bent across your sullen, cold,
Exhausted face? It hurts my heart to watch you,
Deep-shadow'd from the candle's guttering gold;
And you wonder why I shake you by the shoulder;
Drowsy, you mumble and sigh and turn your head . . .
You are too young to fall asleep for ever;
And when you sleep you remind me of the dead.

England, 20th century

The Companion

Yevgeny Yevtushenko

She was sitting on the rough embankment,
her cape too big for her tied on slapdash
over an odd little hat with a bobble on it,
her eyes brimming with tears of hopelessness.
An occasional butterfly floated down
fluttering warm wings onto the rails.
The clinkers underfoot were deep lilac.

252

We got cut off from our grandmothers
while the Germans were dive-bombing the train.
Katya was her name. She was nine.
I'd no idea what I could do about her,
but doubt quickly dissolved to certainty:
I'd have to take this thing under my wing;
—girls were in some sense of the word human,
a human being couldn't just be left.
The droning in the air and the explosions
receded farther into the distance,
I touched the little girl on her elbow.
'Come on. Do you hear? What are you waiting for?'
The world was big and we were not big,
and it was tough for us to walk across it.
She had galoshes on and felt boots,
I had a pair of second-hand boots.
We forded streams and tramped across the forest;
each of my feet at every step it took
taking a smaller step inside the boot.
The child was feeble, I was certain of it,
'Boo-hoo,' she'd say. 'I'm tired,' she'd say.
She'd tire in no time I was certain of it,
but as things turned out it was me who tired.
I growled I wasn't going any further
and sat down suddenly beside the fence.
'What's the matter with you?' she said.
'Don't be so stupid! Put grass in your boots.
Do you want to eat something? Why don't you talk?
Hold this tin, this is crab.
We'll have refreshments. You small boys,
you're always pretending to be brave.'
Then out I went across the prickly stubble
marching beside her in a few minutes.
Masculine pride was muttering in my mind:
I scraped together strength and I held out
for fear of what she'd say. I even whistled.

Grass was sticking out from my tattered boots.
So on and on
we walked without thinking of rest
passing craters, passing fire,
under the rocking sky of '41
tottering crazy on its smoking columns.

U.S.S.R., 20th century
Trans. Milner-Gulland & Levi

O What is that Sound

W. H. Auden

O what is that sound which so thrills the ear
  Down in the valley drumming, drumming?
Only the scarlet soldiers, dear,
  The soldiers coming.

O what is that light I see flashing so clear
  Over the distance brightly, brightly?
Only the sun on their weapons, dear,
  As they step lightly.

O what are they doing with all that gear,
  What are they doing this morning, this morning?
Only the usual manoeuvres, dear,
  Or perhaps a warning.

O why have they left the road down there,
  Why are they suddenly wheeling, wheeling?
Perhaps a change in the orders, dear.
  Why are you kneeling?

O haven't they stopped for the doctor's care,
  Haven't they reined their horses, their horses?
Why, they are none of them wounded, dear,
  None of these forces.

O is it the parson they want, with white hair,
   Is it the parson, is it, is it?
No, they are passing his gateway, dear,
   Without a visit.

O it must be the farmer who lives so near.
   It must be the farmer so cunning, so cunning?
They have passed the farmyard already, dear,
   And now they are running.

O where are you going? Stay with me here!
   Were the vows you swore deceiving, deceiving?
No, I promised to love you, dear,
   But I must be leaving.

O it's broken the lock and splintered the door,
   O it's the gate where they're turning, turning;
Their boots are heavy on the floor
   And their eyes are burning.

                   U.S.A., 20th century

Δώρια
(Doria)

Ezra Pound

Be in me as the eternal moods
   of the bleak wind, and not
As transient things are—
   gaiety of flowers.
Have me in the strong loneliness
   of sunless cliffs
And of grey waters.
   Let the gods speak softly of us
In days hereafter,
   The shadowy flowers of Orcus
Remember thee.

                U.S.A., 20th century

The Twa Corbies

Anon.

As I was walking all a-lane,
I heard twa corbies makin' a–mane.
The tane intae the tither did say,
'Whaur sall we gang and dine the day,
Oh, whaur sall we gang and dine the day?'

'It's in ahint yon auld fail–dyke
I wot there lies a new slain knight;
And naebody kens that he lies there
But his hawk and his hound, and his lady fair, O.
But his hawk and his hound, and his lady fair.

'His hound is to the hunting gane
His hawk to fetch the wild–fowl hame,
His lady's ta'en anither mate,
So we may mak our dinner swate O,
So we may mak our dinner swate.'

'Ye'll sit on his white hause–bane,
And I'll pike oot his bonny blue e'en,
Wi' ae lock o' his gouden hair
We'll theek oor nest when it grows bare, O,
We'll theek oor nest when it grows bare.'

There's mony a ane for him maks mane
But nane sall ken whaur he is gane,
O'er his white banes when they are bare
The wind sall blaw for evermair, O,
The wind sall blaw for evermair.

Scotland, trad.

As He Lay Dying

Randolph Stow

As he lay dying, two fat crows
  Sat perched above in a strangling vine,
    And one crow called to the other:
      'Brother,
    Harvest his eyes, his tongue is mine.'

As he lay dying, two lithe hawks
  Caressed the wind and spied two crows;
    And one hawk hissed to the other:
      'Brother,
    Mine is the sleekest one of those.'

As he lay dying, two eagles passed
  And saw two hawks that hung in flying,
    And one said soft to the other:
      'Brother,
    Mark your prey.' As he lay dying.

Australia, 20th century

The Falcon

Anon.

Lully, lullay! lully, lullay!
The falcon hath borne my make away!

He bare him up, he bare him down,
He bare him into an orchard brown.

In that orchard there was an hall,
That was hangèd with purple and pall.

And in that hall there was a bed,
It was hangèd with gold sa red.

And in that bed there lieth a knight,
His woundès bleeding day and night.

At that bed's foot there lieth a hound,
Licking the blood as it runs down.

By that bed-side kneeleth a may,
And she weepeth both night and day.

And at that bed's head standeth a stone,
Corpus Christi written thereon.

Lully, lullay! lully, lullay!
The falcon hath borne my make away.

England, trad.

A Lyke-Wake Dirge

Anon.

This ae night, this ae night,
Every night and all,
Fire and fleet and candlelight,
And Christ receive thy saule.

When thou from hence away art past,
Every night and all,
To whinny-muir thou com'st at last;
And Christ receive thy saule.

If ever thou gav'st hos'n and shoon,
Every night and all,
Sit thee down and put them on;
And Christ receive thy saule.

If hos'n and shoon thou ne'er gav'st nane,
Every night and all,
The whinnes sall prick thee to the bare bane;
And Christ receive thy saule.

From Whinny-muir when thou may'st pass,
Every night and all,
To Brig o' Dread thou com'st at last;
And Christ receive thy saule.

From Brig o' Dread when thou may'st pass,
Every night and all,
To Purgatory fire thou com'st at last;
And Christ receive thy saule.

If ever thou gav'st meat or drink,
Every night and all,
The fire sall never make thee shrink;
And Christ receive thy saule.

If meat or drink thou ne'er gav'st nane,
Every night and all,
The fire will burn thee to the bare bane;
And Christ receive thy saule.

This ae night, this ae night,
Every night and all,
Fire and fleet and candlelight,
And Christ receive thy saule.

Scotland, trad.

Standing at the foot of the steps at night
Yüan Mei

The bright light of the stars is dimmed;
A few drops of rain begin to fall.
Now the trees know that Autumn approaches,
And softly from leaf to leaf
The news is whispered.

China, 18th century
Trans. D.M.

259

The Wild Swans at Coole

W. B. Yeats

The trees are in their autumn beauty,
The woodland paths are dry,
Under the October twilight the water
Mirrors a still sky;
Upon the brimming water among the stones
Are nine-and-fifty swans.

The nineteenth autumn has come upon me
Since I first made my count;
I saw, before I had well finished,
All suddenly mount
And scatter wheeling in great broken rings
Upon their clamorous wings.

I have looked upon those brilliant creatures,
And now my heart is sore.
All's changed since I, hearing at twilight,
The first time on this shore,
The bell-beat of their wings above my head,
Trod with a lighter tread.

Unwearied still, lover by lover,
They paddle in the cold,
Companionable streams or climb the air;
Their hearts have not grown old;
Passion or conquest, wander where they will,
Attend upon them still.

But now they drift on the still water,
Mysterious, beautiful;
Among what rushes will they build,
By what lake's edge or pool
Delight men's eyes when I awake some day
To find they have flown away?

Ireland, 20th century

from The Georgics

Book I, lines 311–392

Virgil

Am I to tell you next of the storms and stars of autumn?
The things, when days draw in and summer's heat is abating,
That men must guard against? The dangers of showery spring,
When the prick-eared harvest already bristles along the plains
And when in the green blade the milky grain is swelling?
Well, often I've seen a farmer lead into his golden fields
The reapers and begin to cut the frail-stalked barley,
And winds arise that moment, starting a free-for-all,
Tearing up by the roots whole swathes of heavy corn
And hurling them high in the air: with gusts black as a hurricane
The storm sent flimsy blades and stubble flying before it.
Often, too, huge columns of water come in the sky
And clouds charged off the deep amass for dirty weather
With rain-squalls black: then the whole sky gives way, falls,
Floods with terrific rain the fertile crops and the labours
Of oxen; filled are the ditches, dry rivers arise in spate
Roaring, the sea foams and seethes up the hissing fjords.
The Father, enthroned in midnight cloud, hurls from a flashing
Right hand his lightning: the whole
Earth trembles at the shock; the beasts are fled, and human
Hearts are felled in panic throughout the nations: on Athos,
Rhodope or the Ceraunian massif his bolt flares down:
The south wind doubles its force and thicker falls the rain:
Now wail the woods with that gale tremendous, now the shores
    wail.
Fearing this, keep track of the signs and constellations,
Notice whither the cold star of Saturn takes himself
And into what sky-circles Mercury is moving.
Above all, worship the gods, paying your yearly tribute
To the Corn-goddess—a sacrifice on the cheerful grass
Just at the close of winter, when spring has cleared the sky.

Oh then the lambs are fat, then are wines most mellow,
Sweet then is sleep and rich on mountains lie the shadows.
Let all your labouring men worship the Corn-goddess:
For her let the honeycomb be steeped in milk and mild wine,
The mascot led three times round the young crops—a victim
Fêted by all your fellows accompanying it in a body:
Let them call her into their houses
With a shout, and let nobody lay his sickle to the ripe corn
Till in her honour he's placed on his head a wreath of oak leaves
And danced impromptu dances and sung the harvester's hymn.
     So that we might be able to predict from manifest signs
These things—heatwaves and rain and winds that bring cold
          weather,
The Father himself laid down what the moon's phases should mean,
The cue for the south wind's dropping, the sign that often noted
Should warn a farmer to keep his cattle nearer the shippon.
At once, when winds are rising,
The sea begins to fret and heave, and a harsh crackling
Is heard from timbered heights, or a noise that carries far
Comes confused from the beaches, and copses moan crescendo.
At such a time are the waves in no temper to bear your curved
          ship—
A time when gulls are blown back off the deepsea flying
Swift and screeching inland, a time when cormorants
Play on dry land, and the heron
Leaves his haunt in the fens to flap high over the cloud.
Another gale-warning often is given by shooting stars
That streak downsky and blaze a trail through the night's blackness
Leaving a long white wake:
Often light chaff and fallen leaves eddy in the air,
Or feathers play tig skimming along the skin of water.
But when lightning appears from the quarter of the grim north
          wind,
When it thunders to south or west, then all the countryside
Is a-swim with flooded dykes and all the sailors at sea
Close-reef their dripping sails. No, rain need never take us

Unawares: for high-flying cranes will have flown to valley bottoms
To escape the rain as it rises, or else a calf has looked up
At the sky and snuffed the wind with nostrils apprehensive,
Or the tittering swallow has flitted around and around the lake,
And frogs in the mud have croaked away at their old complaint.
Often too from her underground workings the emmet, wearing
A narrow path, bears out her eggs; a giant rainbow
Bends down to drink; rook armies desert their feeding-ground
In a long column, wing-tip to wing-tip, their wings whirring.
Now seabirds after their kind, and birds that about Caÿster's
Asian waterflats grub in the fresh pools, zestfully fling
Showers of spray over their shoulders,
Now ducking their heads in the creeks, scampering now at the
    wavelets,
Making a bustle and frivolous pantomime of washing.
Then the truculent raven full-throated announces rain
As she stalks alone on the dry sand.
Even at night can girls, spinning their wool, be aware
That a storm approaches, for then they behold in the burning lamp
The oil sputter and crumbly mould collect on the wick.

Italy, 1st century B.C.
Trans. from the Latin
by C. Day Lewis

Naitō Meisetsu

The wind blows grey,
The sun sets through
The winter copse.

Japan, 19th century
Trans. Bownas & Thwaite

from Autumn
Vernon Scannell

It is the football season once more
And the back pages of the Sunday papers
Again show the blurred anguish of goalkeepers.

In Maida Vale, Golders Green and Hampstead
Lamps ripen early in the surprising dusk;
They are furred like stale rinds with a fuzz of mist.

The pavements of Kennington are greasy;
The wind smells of burnt porridge in Bayswater,
And the leaves are mushed to silence in the gutter.

The big hotel like an anchored liner
Rides near the park; lit windows hammer the sky.
Like the slow swish of surf the tyres of taxis sigh.

It is a time of year that's to my taste,
Full of spiced rumours, sharp and velutinous flavours,
Dim with the mist that softens the cruel surfaces,
Makes mirrors vague. It is the mist that I most favour.

England, 20th century

Matsuo Bashō

On a bare branch
A rook roosts:
Autumn dusk.

Japan, 17th century
Trans. Bownas & Thwaite

Ōtomo Ōemaru

Then settle, frost!
When the chrysanthemum's gone
No flowers are left.

Japan, 18th century
Trans. Bownas & Thwaite
ed. D.M.

264

The Bridges

Jean-Nicolas-Arthur Rimbaud

Grey crystal skies.
A strange design of bridges,
some straight, others curved,
others again coming down
at oblique angles to the first,
and all these patterns repeating themselves
in the other windings of the canal
that are lit up,
but all of them so long and light
that the banks, laden with domes,
sink and shrink.
Some of these bridges are still covered with hovels.
Others bear masts, signals, fragile parapets.
Minor chords cross each other and fade;
ropes go up from the embankments.
You can make out a red coat,
possibly other clothes and musical instruments.
Are these popular tunes,
snatches from manorial concerts,
left-overs of public anthems?
The water is grey and blue,
wide as an arm of the sea.
    A ray of white light,
falling from high in the sky,
annihilates this make-belief.

France, 19th century
Trans. Oliver Bernard

from November

John Clare

The landscape sleeps in mist from morn till noon;
  And if the sun looks through, 'tis with a face
Beamless and pale and round, as if the moon,
  When done the journey of her nightly race,
  Had found him sleeping, and supplied his place.
For days the Shepherds in the fields may be,
  Nor mark a patch of sky—blindfold they trace,
  The plains, that seem without a bush or tree,
Whistling aloud by guess, to flocks they cannot see.

England, 19th century

Yosa Buson

Scampering over saucers—
The sound of a rat.
Cold, cold.

Japan, 18th century
Trans. Bownas & Thwaite

Fog

Carl Sandburg

The fog comes
on little cat feet.
It sits looking

over harbour and city
on silent haunches
and then moves on.

U.S.A., 20th century

Gunpowder Plot

Vernon Scannell

For days these curious cardboard buds have lain
In brightly coloured boxes. Soon the night
Will come. We pray there'll be no sullen rain
To make these magic orchids flame less bright.

Now in the garden's darkness they begin
To flower: the frenzied whizz of Catherine-wheel
Puts forth its fiery petals and the thin
Rocket soars to burst upon the steel

Bulwark of a cloud. And then the guy,
Absurdly human phoenix, is again
Gulped by greedy flames: the harvest sky
Is flecked with threshed and glittering golden grain.

'Uncle! A cannon! Watch me as I light it!'
The women helter-skelter, squealing high,
Retreat; the paper fuse is quickly lit,
A cat-like hiss, and spit of fire, a sly

Falter, then the air is shocked with blast.
The cannon bangs and in my nostrils drifts
A bitter scent that brings the lurking past
Lurching to my side. The present shifts,

Allows a ten-year memory to walk
Unhindered now; and so I'm forced to hear
The banshee howl of mortar and the talk
Of men who died, am forced to taste my fear.

I listen for a moment to the guns,
The torn earth's grunts, recalling how I prayed.
The past retreats. I hear a corpse's sons—
'Who's scared of bangers!' 'Uncle! John's afraid!'

England, 20th century

The Gunpowder Plot

from The Great Speech of Sir Edward Philips, Knight,
His Majesty's Sergeant at law, made in Westminster Hall
Monday, January 27th 1606

They, the Conspirators,
all grounded Romanists and corrupted scholars
of so irreligious and traitorous a school,
conspired together in secrecy
receiving the sacrament binding them to their purpose.

Robert Catesby, man of strength, wrong-headed
and desperate almost to madness
by the persecution of the Catholics,
was their leader:
   'Are we not sorely tried and unjustly treated
   and driven like dogs
   to bite back at our savage masters?
   You shall swear by the Blessed Trinity,
   and by the sacrament
   you do now propose to receive,
   never to disclose, directly or undirectly
   by word or circumstance,
   the matter that shall be proposed to you to keep secret—
   nor desert from the execution thereof
   until the rest shall give you leave.'

The Matter Conspired was
First: To Deprive the King of his Rights.
Secondly: To Murder the King, the Queen, and the Prince.
Thirdly: To Stir Rebellion and Sedition in the Kingdom.
Fourthly: To Bring a Miserable Destruction among the Sub-
           jects.
Fifthly: To Change, Alter, and Subvert the Religion here
           Established.
Sixthly: To Ruinate the State of the Commonwealth and to
           bring in strangers to invade it.

The Mean to Effect it they concluded to be that
First: The King, the Queen, the Prince,
             The Lords Spiritual and Temporal,
             The Knights and Burgesses of the Parliament
             should be blown up with powder.
Secondly: That the whole Royal Male Issue should be destroyed.
Thirdly: That they would take into their custody
             the King's daughters Elizabeth and Mary
             and proclaim the Lady Elizabeth Queen. . . .

And Parliament, being promulgated till 7th of February,
and then further adjourned till 3rd October,
they, in Lent, hired a vault, and placed therein
twenty barrels of powder.
On 20th July they laid in more
ten barrels of powder, laying upon them
divers great bars of iron and pieces of timber
and great massive stones
and covering the same with faggots.

On 20th September they laid in more
four hogsheads of powder
with other stones and bars of iron thereon.
On the day before Parliament was to meet,
November 4th, everything was ready.
They stood waiting the moment of their making
which was quietly unmade
by one of them of tender conscience
warning Lord Mounteagle:
                       'to devise some excuse
to shift of your attendance at this Parliament:
for God and man have concurred
to punish the wickedness of this time. . . .
For though there be no appearance of any stir
yet I say they shall receive a terrible blow, this parliament,

and yet they shall not see who hurt them . . . '

This letter
being shown to the King,
was taken to conceal a plot.

It was then resolved
that the houses and rooms around the Parliament House
should be searched.
And that same evening the Lord Chamberlain,
accompanied by Lord Mounteagle, Sir Thomas Knevett,
and others,
proceeded to view a house where they found
in a vault underground
a great store of billets, faggots and coal,
brought, they were told, for the use of Mr Piercy;
and they espied Fawkes standing in a corner of the cellar,
who said that he was Mr Piercy's servant
and left there by him for the keeping of the house.
'Mr Piercy likes a little winter comfort'
said Sir Thomas Knevett.
'Aye, Sir!' Fawkes replied.

Upon the naming of Piercy,
Lord Mounteagle told the Chamberlain
that he suspected Piercy to be the author of the letter,
and it was resolved that further search should be made
what was that great pile of fuel in such a house
where Piercy had so little occasion to reside.

At midnight, Sir Thomas Knevett
with a small party of armed men, repaired thither
and found Fawkes standing at the door
booted and spurred, whom he at once apprehended.
Upon him were three matches,
a tinder-box, and a dark lantern.

The king was informed of it
as well as the Privy Council,
while the arch traitor was brought to the Tower of London.

.   .   .

The Executions
as reported in The Weekley Newes, Friday 31st January 1606

Now, after their condemnation and judgement
the Conspirators were sent again
to the Tower of London.
And when the day of execution arrived
they were drawn upon sledges and hurdles
into Saint Paul's Churchyard, four of them,
Digby, the elder Winter, Graunt, and Bates.
And when they were hanged the executioners
prepared to draw and quarter them;
and when this was done
the business of the day was ended.

The next day being Friday, were drawn from the Tower
to the Old Palace Yard in Westminster
Thomas Winter, Rookewood, Keyes, and Fawkes.

Winter went first up the scaffold;
with a very pale face, and dead colour,
he went up the ladder
and after a swing or two with the halter,
to the quartering block was drawn,
and there quickly despatched.

Next came Rookewood . . .
And then came Keyes . . .

Last of all came the great Devil of all,
Guy Fawkes, alias Johnson,
who should have put fire to the powder.

His body being weak
with the torture and sickness,
he was scarce able to go up the ladder.
Yet, with much ado,
by the help of the hangman,
went high enough to break his neck by the fall.

He made no speech
but with his crosses and idle ceremonies
made his end upon the gallows and the block,
to the great joy of all beholders
that the land was ended of so wicked a villainy.

England, 17th century
Arr. D.M.

from The Tragedy of King Lear

William Shakespeare

Blow, winds, and crack your cheeks! rage! blow!
You cataracts and hurricanoes, spout
Till you have drenched our steeples, drowned the cocks!
You sulphurous and thought-executing fires,
Vaunt-couriers to oak-cleaving thunderbolts,
Singe my white head! And thou, all-shaking thunder,
Smite flat the thick rotundity o' the world!
Crack nature's moulds, all germins spill at once
That make ingrateful man!

England, 16th century

Takahama Kyoshi

On far hills
The sun catches:
Bleak moorland.

Japan, 20th century
Trans. Bownas & Thwaite

Takahama Kyoshi

Against the broad sky
Stretching and leaning,
Winter trees.

Japan, 20th century
Trans. Bownas & Thwaite

Ancient Music

Ezra Pound

Winter is icummen in,
Lhude sing Goddamm,
Raineth drop and staineth slop,
And how the wind doth ramm!
    Sing: Goddamm.
Skiddeth bus and sloppeth us,
An ague hath my ham.
Freezeth river, turneth liver,
    Damn you, sing: Goddamm.
Goddamm, Goddamm, 'tis why I am, Goddamm,
    So 'gainst the winter's balm.
Sing goddamm, damm, sing Goddamm,
Sing goddamm, sing goddamm, DAMM.

U.S.A., 20th century

273

Bare Almond-Trees

D. H. Lawrence

Wet almond-trees, in the rain,
Like iron sticking grimly out of earth;
Black almond trunks, in the rain,
Like iron implements twisted, hideous, out of the
    earth,
Out of the deep, soft fledge of Sicilian winter-green,
Earth-grass uneatable,
Almond trunks curving blackly, iron-dark, climbing
    the slopes.

Almond-tree, beneath the terrace rail,
Black, rusted, iron trunk,
You have welded your thin stems finer,
Like steel, like sensitive steel in the air,
Grey, lavender, sensitive steel, curving thinly and
    brittly up in a parabola.

What are you doing in the December rain?
Have you a strange electric sensitiveness in your steel
    tips?
Do you feel the air for electric influences
Like some strange magnetic apparatus?
Do you take in messages, in some strange code,
For heaven's wolfish, wandering electricity, that
    prowls so constantly round Etna?
Do you take the whisper of sulphur from the air?
Do you hear the chemical accents of the sun?
Do you telephone the roar of the waters over the
    earth?
And from all this, do you make calculations?

Sicily, December's Sicily in a mass of rain
With iron branching blackly, rusted like old, twisted
    implements
And brandishing and stooping over earth's wintry
    fledge, climbing the slopes
Of uneatable soft green!

England, 20th century

from Snow Storm

John Clare

What a night! The wind howls, hisses, and but stops
To howl more loud, while the snow volley keeps
Incessant batter at the window pane,
Making our comfort feel as sweet again;
And in the morning, when the tempest drops,
At every cottage door mountainous heaps
Of snow lie drifted, that all entrance stops
Until the beesom and the shovel gain
The path, and leave a wall on either side.

England, 19th century

Stopping by Woods on a Snowy Evening

Robert Frost

Whose woods these are I think I know.
His house is in the village though;
He will not see me stopping here
To watch his woods fill up with snow.

My little horse must think it queer
To stop without a farmhouse near
Between the woods and frozen lake
The darkest evening of the year.

He gives his harness bells a shake
To ask if there is some mistake.
The only other sound's the sweep
Of easy wind and downy flake.

The woods are lovely, dark and deep,
But I have promises to keep,
And miles to go before I sleep,
And miles to go before I sleep.

U.S.A., 20th century

Kobayashi Issa

I could eat it!
This snow that falls
  So softly, so softly.

Japan, 19th century
Trans. R. H. Blyth

Now Winter Nights Enlarge

Thomas Campion

Now winter nights enlarge
The number of their hours,
And clouds their storms discharge
Upon the airy towers.
Let now the chimneys blaze,
And cups o'erflow with wine;
Let well-tuned words amaze
With harmony divine.
Now yellow waxen lights
Shall wait on honey love,
While youthful revels, masques and courtly
 sights
Sleep's leaden spells remove.

This time doth well dispense
With lovers' long discourse;
Much speech hath some defence,
Though beauty no remorse.
All do not all things well;
Some measures comely tread,
Some knotted riddles tell,
Some poems smoothly read.
The summer hath his joys
And winter his delights;
Though love and all his pleasures are
 but toys,
They shorten tedious nights.

England, 16th century

Somewhere Around Christmas

John Smith

Always, or nearly always, on old apple trees,
Somewhere around Christmas, if you look up through
    the frost,
You will see, fat as a bullfinch, stuck on a high branch,
One, lingering, bald, self sufficient, hard, blunt fruit.

There will be no leaves, you can be sure of that;
The twigs will be tar-black, and the white sky
Will be grabbed among the branches like thumbed glass
In broken triangles just saved from crashing to the ground.

Further up, dribbles of rain will run down
Like spilt colourless varnish on a canvas. The old tins,
Tyres, cardboard boxes, debris of back gardens,
Will lie around, bleak, with mould and rust creeping
    over them.

Blow on your fingers. Wipe your feet on the mat by the
    back door.
You will never see that apple fall. Look at the cat,
Her whiskers twitch as she sleeps by the kitchen fire;
In her backyard prowling dream she thinks it's a bird.

England, 20th century

Christmas Landscape

Laurie Lee

Tonight the wind gnaws
with teeth of glass,
the jackdaw shivers
in caged branches of iron,
the stars have talons.

There is hunger in the mouth
of vole and badger,
silver agonies of breath
in the nostrils of the fox,
ice on the rabbit's paw.

Tonight has no moon,
no food for the pilgrim;
the fruit tree is bare,
the rose bush a thorn
and the ground bitter with stones.

But the mole sleeps, and the hedgehog
lies curled in a womb of leaves,
the bean and the wheat-seed
hug their germs in the earth
and the stream moves under the ice.

Tonight there is no moon,
but a new star opens
like a silver trumpet over the dead.
Tonight in a nest of ruins
the blessed babe is laid.

And the fir tree warms to a bloom of candles,
the child lights his lantern,
stares at his tinselled toy;
our hearts and hearths
smoulder with live ashes.

In the blood of our grief
the cold earth is suckled,
in our agony the womb
convulses its seed,
in the cry of anguish
the child's first breath is born.

England, 20th century

Hot Cake

Shu Hsi

Winter has come; fierce is the cold;
In the sharp morning air new-risen we meet.
Rheum freezes in the nose;
Frost hangs about the chin.
For hollow bellies, for chattering teeth and
     shivering knees
What better than hot cake?
Soft as the down of spring,
Whiter than autumn floss!
Dense and swift the steam
Rises, swells and spreads.
Fragrance flies through the air,
Is scattered far and wide,
Steals down along the wind and wets
The covetous mouth of passer-by.
Servants and grooms
Throw sidelong glances, munch the empty air.
They lick their lips who serve;
While lines of envious lackeys by the wall
Stand dryly swallowing.

China, 3rd century
Trans. Arthur Waley

Sheep in Winter

John Clare

The sheep get up and make their many tracks
And bear a load of snow upon their backs,
And gnaw the frozen turnip to the ground
With sharp quick bite, and then go noising round
The boy that pecks the turnips all the day

And knocks his hands to keep the cold away
And laps his legs in straw to keep them warm
And hides behind the hedges from the storm.
The sheep, as tame as dogs, go where he goes
And try to shake their fleeces from the snows,
Then leave their frozen meal and wander round
The stubble stack that stands beside the ground,
And lie all night and face the drizzling storm
And shun the hovel where they might be warm.

England, 19th century

In Freezing Winter Night

Robert Southwell

Behold, a silly tender babe,
In freezing winter night,
In homely manger trembling lies;
Alas, a piteous sight!
The inns are full; no man will yield
This little pilgrim bed,
But forced he is with silly beasts
In crib to shroud his head. . . .
This stable is a Prince's court,
This crib his chair of state;
The beasts are parcel of his pomp,
The wooden dish his plate.
The persons in that poor attire
His royal liveries wear;
The Prince himself is come from heaven;
This pomp is prizèd there.
With joy approach, O Christian wight,
Do homage to thy King;
And highly praise his humble pomp,
Which he from heaven doth bring.

England, 16th century

Christmas Star

Boris Pasternak

It was winter.
The wind blew from the steppe
And it was cold for the child
In the cave on the hillside.

He was warmed by the breath of an ox.
The farm animals
Were stabled in the cave,
And a warm haze drifted over the manger.

Shaking from their sheepskins
The wisps of straw and hay-seeds of their bedding,
Half asleep, the shepherds gazed
From a rock ledge into the midnight distance.

Far away were a snowy field, a graveyard,
Fences, tombstones,
The shaft of a cart in a snowdrift,
And above the graveyard the sky full of stars.

Near, never seen till then, more shy
Than the glimmer in the window
Of a watchman's hut,
The star shone on its way to Bethlehem.

It flamed like a hayrick,
Standing aside from the sky
And from God;
Glowed like a farm on fire,

Rose like a blazing
Stack of straw.
The sight of the new star
Startled the universe.

Its reddening glow
Was a sign; the three star-gazers
Hurried to the call
Of its unprecedented light.

Camels followed them loaded with gifts,
And donkeys in harness, one smaller than the other,
Minced down the hill.

In a strange vision all time to come
Arose in the distance:
All the thoughts, hopes, worlds of the centuries,
The future of art galleries and of museums,
All the pranks of goblins and deeds of magicians,
All the Christmas trees and all the children's dreams:

The shimmering candles, the paper chains,
The splendour of coloured tinsel . . .
. . . Angrier and more wicked blew the wind from the
        steppe . . .
. . . All the apples and golden bubbles.

Part of the pond was hidden by the alders,
But from where the shepherds stood
A part could be seen between the rooks' nests in the
        treetops.
They watched camels and donkeys skirting the pool.
'Let's go with the others,' they said,
Wrapping themselves in their sheepskins,
'Let's bow to the miracle.'

They grew hot from shuffling in the snow.
On the bright plain bare footsteps,
Shining like glass, led round the hut.
In the starlight the sheep-dogs growled at these tracks,
As though they were burning candle-ends.

The frosty night was like a fairy-tale.
Invisible beings kept stepping down
From the snowdrifts into the crowd.

The dogs followed, looking round apprehensively;
They kept close to the youngest shepherd, expecting
      trouble.

Through the same countryside, along the same road,
Several angels walked among the crowd.
Bodiless beings, they were invisible;
Only their steps left a trace.

A crowd had gathered by the stone at the entrance.
Day was breaking. The trunks of the cedars were plain.
'Who are you?' asked Mary.
'We are a company of shepherds and envoys from
      heaven.
We have come to praise you both.'
'You can't all come in at once. Wait a little by the
      door.'

Shepherds and herdsmen stamped about
In the ashy dusk before the dawn.
By the wooden water trough
Men on foot and horsemen swore at each other,
Camels roared and asses kicked.

Day was breaking. The dawn swept the remaining stars
Like cinders from the sky.
Out of all the great gathering Mary allowed
Only the Wise Men through the opening in the rock.

He slept in the oak manger,
Radiant as moonlight in the hollow of a tree.
Instead of a sheepskin,
The lips of the ass and the nostrils of the ox kept him warm.

The Magi stood in the shadow,
Whispering, scarcely finding words.
All at once, a hand stretched out of the dark,
Moved one of them aside to the left of the manger:
He looked round. Gazing at the Virgin from the doorway
Like a guest, was the Christmas Star.

U.S.S.R., 20th century
Trans. Lydia Pasternak

Carol

W. R. Rodgers

Deep in the fading leaves of light
There lay the flower that darkness knows,
Till winter stripped and brought to light
The most incomparable Rose
That blows, that blows.

The flashing mirrors of the snow
Keep turning and returning still:
To see the lovely child below
And hold him is their only will;
Keep still, keep still.

And to let go his very cry
The clinging echoes are so slow
That still his wail they multiply
Though he lie singing now below,
So low, so low.

Even the doves forget to grieve
And gravely to his greeting fly.
And the lone places that they leave
All follow and are standing by
On high, on high.

Ireland, 20th century

e. e. cummings

little tree
little silent Christmas tree
you are so little
you are more like a flower

who found you in the green forest
and were you very sorry to come away?
see   i will comfort you
because you smell so sweetly

i will kiss your cool bark
and hug you safe and tight
just as your mother would,
only don't be afraid

look   the spangles
that sleep all the year in a dark box
dreaming of being taken out and allowed to shine,
the balls the chains red and gold the fluffy threads,

put up your little arms
and i'll give them all to you to hold
every finger shall have its ring
and there won't be a single place dark or unhappy

then when you're quite dressed
you'll stand in the window for everyone to see
and how they'll stare!
oh but you'll be very proud

and my little sister and i will take hands
and looking up at our beautiful tree
we'll dance and sing
'Noel Noel'

U.S.A., 20th century

from The Witnesses

Clive Sansom

The Innkeeper's wife:
　　It was a night in winter.
Our house was full, tight-packed as salted herrings—
So full, they said, we had to hold our breaths
To close the door and shut the night-air out!
And then two travellers came. They stood outside
Across the threshold, half in the ring of light
And half beyond it. I would have let them in
Despite the crowding—the woman was past her time—
But I'd no mind to argue with my husband,
The flagon in my hand and half the inn
Still clamouring for wine. But when trade slackened,
And all our guests had sung themselves to bed
Or told the floor their troubles, I came out here
Where he had lodged them. The man was standing
As you are now, his hand smoothing that board.
He was a carpenter, I heard them say.
She rested on the straw, and on her arm
A child was lying. None of your creased-faced brats
Squalling their lungs out. Just lying there
As calm as a new-dropped calf—his eyes wide open,
And gazing round as if the world he saw
In the chaff-strewn light of the stable lantern
Was something beautiful and new and strange.

England, 20th century

287

The Burning Babe

Robert Southwell

As I in hoary winter's night stood shivering in the snow,
Surprised I was with sudden heat which made my heart to glow;
And lifting up a fearful eye to view what fire was near,
A pretty babe all burning bright did in the air appear;
Who, scorchèd with excessive heat, such floods of tears did shed
As though his floods should quench his flames which with his tears
    were fed.
'Alas,' quoth he, 'but newly born in fiery heats I fry,
Yet none approach to warm their hearts or feel my fire but I!
My faultless breast the furnace is, the fuel wounding thorns,
Love is the fire, and sighs the smoke, the ashes shame and scorns;
The fuel justice layeth on, and mercy blows the coals,
The metal in this furnace wrought are men's defilèd souls,
For which, as now on fire I am to work them to their good,
So will I melt into a bath to wash them in my blood.'
With this he vanished out of sight and swiftly shrunk away,
And straight I callèd unto mind that it was Christmas day.

England, 16th century

As Dew in Aprille

Anon.

I sing of a maiden
That is makèles:
King of all kings
To her son she ches.
He came al so stille
There his moder was,
As dew in Aprille
That falleth on the grass.

288

He came al so stille,
To his moder's bour,
As dew in Aprille
That falleth on the flour.
He came al so stille
There his moder lay,
As dew in Aprille
That falleth on the spray.
Moder and mayden
Was never none but she,
Well may such a lady
Goddes moder be.

England, medieval

When You Are Old

W. B. Yeats

When you are old and grey and full of sleep,
And nodding by the fire, take down this book,
And slowly read, and dream of the soft look
Your eyes had once, and of their shadows deep;

How many loved your moments of glad grace,
And loved your beauty with love false or true,
But one man loved the pilgrim soul in you,
And loved the sorrows of your changing face;

And bending down beside the glowing bars,
Murmur, a little sadly, how Love fled
And paced upon the mountains overhead
And hid his face amid a crowd of stars.

Ireland, 20th century

Stars, Songs, Faces

Carl Sandburg

Gather the stars if you wish it so.
Gather the songs and keep them.
Gather the faces of women.
Gather for keeping years and years.
   And then . . .
Loosen your hands, let go and say good-bye.
   Let the stars and songs go.
   Let the faces and years go.
   Loosen your hands and say good-bye.

U.S.A., 20th century

NOTES AND INDEXES

Notes

[1] Compare this modern translation from The Anchor Bible (Doubleday, 1964) with that of the Authorised version (The King James Bible) of 1611.

[3] A very old carol that was once sung from house to house. Even without music it is cheerful and bright to listen to.

[4] and [5] A Welsh poet and an English poet celebrate the bleakness of winter. Aneirin paints a depressing picture of life in the sixth century, when food supplies had run out. Thirteen centuries later, Clare celebrates the first sign of spring—in spite of the weather— much as we would today.

[5] A poem that, in the depth of winter's cold, begs for sun. Benjamin Britten used it in the first movement of his Spring Symphony, and his music recreates the chilling effects of the poem's images.

[6] And when the sun *does* come, the poet sings with a different voice: both Nashe and Surrey fill their poems with careful observation of nature. *Soote*, sweet; *eke*, also; *pale*, stake, or fence; *mings*, mixes; *bale*, an evil, fatal influence, inflicting death.

[7] 'By chance I walk . . .' This poem appears in another translation in *The Moment of Wonder* edited by Richard Lewis (Dial Press, New York, 1964), a collection of translations of poems from China and Japan, beautifully illustrated with Chinese and Japanese paintings and drawings.

[7] e. e. cummings always wrote his name without capitals. His poems are sometimes wayward too in their appearance. He has a surprising, new way of putting together quite ordinary words and with them creates a special magic and mystery.

293

[8] 'Winter withering' is a haiku, a special poetic form used in Japan. A haiku has three lines: the first has five syllables, the next seven, and the third five—seventeen syllables in all. Almost always the poem ends with a noun and contains some reference to a season of the year. It is a subtle mixture of unchanging things and of something seen or heard or felt for no more than a moment. The last line brings these two together. In this way, writes Geoffrey Bownas, the poet attempts to 'capture in his verses a vision into the nature of the world'. These visions, as Richard Lewis puts it, 'come and go in a glance'. A Japanese collector of poetry, Ki Tsurayuki, wrote: 'Poetry has its seeds in man's heart. ... When we hear the notes of the nightingale among the blossoms, when we hear the frog in the water, we know that every living being is capable of song. Poetry, without effort, can move heaven and earth, can touch the gods and spirits ... it turns the hearts of man and woman to each other and it soothes the soul of the fierce warrior.'

Why seventeen syllables? Nobuyuki Yuasa, in his translation of Bashō's *The Narrow Road to the Deep North* (Penguin Books, 1964) writes: 'the Japanese language falls most naturally into breathing groups of five or seven syllables.' Here, as an example, is a haiku by Bashō, one of the greatest writers of the haiku.

F u r u i k e y a,	An old silent pond,
1 2 3 4 5	
K a w a z u t o b i k o m u —	A frog jumps into the
1 2 3 4 5 6 7	water—
m i z u n o o t o.	A deep note sounds.
1 2 3 4 5	

The sounds of words and the special ways in which words are put together never pass easily from one language into another. It is never possible for a translator exactly to capture in a foreign language the way in which a writer uses his own language. The translator must make a new poem in the foreign language, and thus must attempt both to reflect the original and remain true to the special qualities of the language in which the translation is made. The translator, then, must also be a poet.

The most complete study of the haiku is to be found in four volumes under the general title *Haiku* by R. H. Blyth (The Hokuseido Press, Tokyo, 1947–52). (1) *Eastern Culture*; (2) *Spring*; (3) *Summer—Autumn*; (4) *Autumn—Winter*.

Many haikai are included in *The Moment of Wonder* (see note to p. 7), and in *The Penguin Book of Japanese Verse* translated by Geoffrey Bownas and Anthony Thwaite (Penguin Books, 1964). In *Once Around the Sun* edited by Brian Thompson (Oxford University Press, 1966) are to be found examples of 'English' haikai written by Australian children.

[9] Like their Elizabethan counterparts, Chinese court and government officials wrote poetry. In this they were doing what was expected of the well-born. Po Chü-i was, in 825, Governor of Soochow. The translator of this poem, Arthur Waley, was chiefly responsible for enabling English readers to know something of Chinese poetry. Of Po Chü-i he wrote: 'I find him by far the most translatable of the major Chinese poets.' See also 'Pruning Trees', p. 107. Books by Arthur Waley include: *The Book of Songs* (Allen & Unwin, 2nd impression 1968), *Chinese Poems* (Allen & Unwin, 1946).

In *A Collection of Chinese Lyrics* rendered into verse by Alan Ayling from translations by Duncan Mackintosh (Routledge & Kegan Paul, 1965) you will find the Chinese originals handwritten by Lee Yin.

Three books, published by Penguin Books, are readily available: *The Penguin Book of Chinese Verse*, verse translations by Robert Kotewall and Norman L. Smith, introduced and edited by A. R. Davis (1962); *Poems and the Late T'ang*, translated with an introduction by A. C. Graham (1965); *Anthology of Chinese Literature from Earliest Times to the Fourteenth Century*, compiled and edited by Cyril Birch, Associate Editor Donald Keene (1967).

[10] John Clare, the countryman born a poet, spent his life recording the beauty of nature. He was not well schooled: he could not spell very well and almost never punctuated his poems. This has been done for him by the editors of his work.

Sadly, Clare spent the last twenty-two years of his life in a lunatic asylum, where he wrote many of his finest poems. A selection of his work, *The Wood is Sweet* (Bodley Head, 1966), has been made specially for young readers by David Powell.

[11] Virgil is most famous for his long epic poem *The Aeneid*; he also wrote poems about the countryside called *The Eclogues*, and the poem about farming from which this (and other) extracts are taken, *The Georgics*. C. Day Lewis, the Poet Laureate, has translated the poem into English verse which catches something of the sublimity of the original Latin.

[16, 17] Geoffrey Chaucer (?1340–1400) is the first great English poet. He is also a great story teller. *The Canterbury Tales* is a collection of old stories re-told in verse. Each story is put into the mouth of one of a group of pilgrims on their way to Canterbury. Chaucer's plan was for each to tell two stories on the way there, and two on the return journey. Thus would they pass the time without getting bored. Indeed, although he did not complete the plan, he is as good as his word. He writes with masterly ease and clarity, is comic and serious by turns, and throughout his writing shows his deep understanding of human nature.

The English language, like all living languages, is constantly changing. In the six centuries since Chaucer lived it has changed a good deal, but not so much that we do not readily recognise the language of *The Canterbury Tales* as English. Here you can compare the original with the translation into modern English made by Nevill Coghill (Penguin Books, 1951).

Zephyrus, the west wind; *pricks*, excites; *palmers*, pilgrims who have been to the Holy Land; *the holy blissful martyr*, Thomas Becket, Archbishop of Canterbury, who was murdered by four of King Henry II's knights in 1170; for three hundred years the worship of St. Thomas the Martyr was a popular cult and many people went to Canterbury to seek out his tomb. The word *canter* is derived from 'Canterbury gallop', the pace of the horses on which the pilgrims rode; *Stratford-atte-Bowe*, Stratford, East London; *palfrey*, horse; *sanguine*, of a ruddy complexion, and by nature, courageous, hopeful and confident; *Epicurus*, an Athenian philosopher who disbelieved in the divine government of the world and in a future life; *epicure*, one who likes a life of pleasure, especially eating; *seethe*, stew; *broil*, to boil up all ingredients together; *vintner*, wine merchant; *astronomy*, the scientific study of heavenly bodies—but here the word implies also the prediction of events by the observation of the position of stars, the study which is now known as astrology: mediaeval medical men believed that men's health was influenced by the stars; *seat*, the place in which a disease was to be found; *humour*, one of the four chief fluids of the body (blood, phlegm, choler or bile, and melancholy or black bile—which gave rise to bad temper and depression); *condition*, the state of the disease; *so wrath was she*, so angry was she, she lost her temper; *well wimpled up*, her head was covered with a wimple, a head-covering which enveloped her head, chin, cheeks and neck, now worn only by nuns; *a clerk*, a member of the five 'minor orders' of the church as distinct from 'holy orders', sometimes used to refer to a man who could read and write, especially at a time when most people could do neither; *scrupulosity*, doubts or scruples of conscience, he never indulged in arguments about what he believed; *lore*, teachings; *wrangler and buffoon*, one quick to pick a quarrel or argument and one who jests, ridicules and plays the fool.

[34] 'Cuccu Song': this song is at least a century earlier than Chaucer, but it is still sung today in many schools. It is used by Benjamin Britten in the final movement of his Spring Symphony. There are modernised versions of the song, but these take away some of the flavour and rhythm of the original. It is printed here in its original form. *Sed*, seed; *bloweth med*, the fields break into flower (buttercups and daisies, perhaps); *wude*, woods, trees; *nu*, now (in some parts of the British Isles, *now* is still pronounced *noo*); *awe*, ewe, but note that in this word, as in *lhude*, *wude*, *calve*, *bucke*, the final *e* is pronounced; *bleteth*, bleats; *lomb*, lamb; *lhouth*, lows, calls; *bulluc sterteth*, the bullock leaps and jumps (compare Chaucer's use of the word *priketh* to describe how excitable all creatures are in the spring); *murie*, merrily; *ne swike thu naver nu*, do not ever stop now. Notice the double negative which in modern standard English has disappeared. In a literal translation it might read: *nor stop you never now*. In some dialects, like

Cockney, the negative with the two elements still exists. In this, Cockney is like French and Russian.

[35] *cliché*, an expression which through frequent exact repetition loses its effectiveness; *lambent threat*, the threat in the sudden flashes of the lightning; *Miss Davies*, the Sunday School teacher.

[37] *brunt*, attacking, more commonly found in the expression *to bear the brunt of*.

[39] *hierarchies*, ranked in order, one above the other. The story of Noah and the ark is to be found in the Book of Genesis, Chapters 6–8.

[42] *gout*, painful inflammation of the smaller joints, especially the big toe; *ague*, acute fever accompanied by hot and cold shivering.

[45] Beowulf is the hero of this Early English poem. He travelled to Denmark to rid Hrothgar's kingdom of the man-eating monster called Grendel. The poem was originally composed and first written down in Anglo-Saxon, or Old English. This was a Germanic language brought to England after the Romans left, and for seven centuries it remained the language of England— until the Norman conquest in the eleventh century. Anglo-Saxon poetry is serious and heroic, and the feelings it expresses are often deep and violent. The unknown poet of *Beowulf* would have recited his poem (accompanying himself with the harp) to an assembled audience. They would have been used to listening to such poetry. In his performance the poet was bound only by the rules of poetry-making and he was free to change details of the story, so probably no two performances would have been alike. This poem is best listened to, but the reader should note the two main stresses in each line, which are placed on either side of a pause. Anglo-Saxon poetry makes great use of alliteration— as does the work of Gerard Manley Hopkins. Further extracts from Anglo-Saxon poetry are to be found in *The Earliest English Poems*, translated by Michael Alexander (Penguin Books, 1962), and there is a translation of the whole poem of *Beowulf* by David Wright (Penguin Books, 1957).

[46] 'Sir Patrick Spens' is one of the most popular of all the ballads. It is not known for certain whether the story of the voyage and the

subsequent shipwreck is taken from historical fact, or whether it was written simply as a literary 'piece'. The name Sir Patrick Spens has not yet been traced in any historical document. However, there are two sources from which the idea for the poem may have sprung. The first is the journey of Margaret of Norway to Scotland in 1281. Many ships escorted her, and some of these foundered and sank with the loss of all their crew. Later, Margaret's daughter, The Maid of Norway, was drowned when the ships bringing her to England to marry Edward I sank in a storm.

The version here is that found in Thomas Percy's *Reliques of Ancient English Poetry*, where his name is given as Sir Patrick Spence. The ballad should be spoken by a Scot in order to realise its full beauty. The spelling of the original has been retained so as to give some clues to pronunciation. *richt*, right; *braid*, broad, plain, obvious; *lauch*, laugh; *teir*, tear; *quha*, who; *yeir*, year; *the morne*, tomorrow morning; *yestreen*, last night; *laith*, reluctant; *weet*, wet; *schoone*, shoes; *lang owre*, long before; *aboone*, above; *or e'er*, before; *kems*, combs; *ne mair*, no more; *owre*, over.

[53] The two poems written to the title 'Looking at the moon on putting out from the shore at Nagato', are known by the name of *tanka*. Haiku and tanka are still written today by Japanese—not only by professional poets but also by farmers, business men, shop assistants, engineers and students. A tanka (short poem) is like a little song, private and personal to the writer. It is frequently made up of thirty-one syllables in five lines of five, seven, five, seven, seven syllables.

Nagato is near the town of Hiroshima which was totally destroyed by an atom bomb at the end of the Second World War.

[56] A visual wordless poem, witty and elegant, in which the ripples on the water, the indication of the shape of the fish's mouth in breathing, of its being open-eyed, are all combined—with the hint of a contented smile.

Poems which exploit visually the arrangement of words and typographical symbols on a page are to be found in *Apollinaire, Selected Poems*, translated with an introduction by Oliver Ber-

nard (Penguin Books, 1965). In Chapter 3 of *Alice in Wonderland*,
Lewis Carroll wrote a poem out of a mouse's tail. There are two
versions—that beginning 'we lived beneath the mat' is the better.
See *The Annotated Alice*, edited by Martin Gardner, pages 50 and
51 (Penguin Books, 1965).

[58] The poet Karai Senryū gave his name to a seventeen-syllable
poem (senryū) in which the writer is free to write about everyday
happenings and feelings. In this way it differs from the stricter
form, the haiku.

[78] The Chester Miracle Play, of which this is a shortened version,
and in which the spelling has been modernised, is based on
part of Chapter 22 of the Book of Genesis, verses 1–18. The
purpose of this play and of others like it, was to enable the
illiterate people of the Middle Ages to understand the Bible
stories. In church they heard these read in Latin and were un-
likely to understand them any more than many people would
today. The plays were made and performed in homely conditions
and were watched in the street. They display the natural dramatic
sense of unsophisticated people and their sense of humour and
pathos. Into these versions of biblical texts are woven details of
local language and character which make them more English
than Jewish.

full beane, very willing; *fain*, gladly; *bayne*, obedient; *middle
earde*, middle earth, i.e. the earth as placed between heaven and
hell; *yard*, stick; *lean*, hide; *wot*, know; *i-wiss*, surely; *wether*, a
ram; *anon*, at once; *heigh*, have; *bonere*, good; *leve*, believe.

[92] These lines (with the exception of the first) appear in the short
story by Glyn Jones, *Porth-y-Rhyd*, from his collection of short
stories *The Blue Bed* (Jonathan Cape, 1937). They have been
rearranged by Hugh MacDiarmid to make the poem which he
has called 'Perfect'. *machair*, foreshore.

[136] A selection of Blake's poems has been chosen and introduced for
young readers by Rosemary Manning under the title, *A Grain
of Sand* (Bodley Head, 1967).

[146] The true ballad is a folk-story told in song. It is meant to be performed in public, not read in a book. Yet, even without music, the best ballads can have as powerful an effect on the reader as on the listener. In them action and situation are of first importance, so they are often sensational and violent. The stories they tell are little dramas in which the characters are much less important than the plot.

There are a number of versions of 'Young Beichan', each differing from the others in some details. In this version the spelling has been modernised.

Mahound, Mohammed, the prophet; *Termagant*, an imaginary god thought by Christians of the Middle Ages to have been worshipped by Mohammedans, represented in mystery plays as a savage and proud personage; stanza 3 is a description of Young Beichan in slavery, yoked so as to pull loads of spices and wine; *e'e*, eyes; *stown*, stolen; *mickle*, much; *white money*, silver; *wot*, know; *malvoisie*, Malmsey, a strong, sweet wine, *a'*, all; *yon*, that; *kye*, cows; *ha'*, hall; *'yond*, beyond; *tirlèd softly at the pin*, rattled the lock; *won up*, get up; *mote*, must; *dreed*, suffered.

[156] This ballad is incomplete, but in this version an attempt has been made to conceal the fact that some stanzas have been lost. There is, for example, no explanation for the treachery of Robin's cousin, the Prioress.

bleed, to draw or let blood from the body (especially of one who was ill) in the belief that with the escape of blood the illness would be brought out of the body. (Blood was one of the four cardinal humours believed in by medieval doctors, see note to p. 16.) *wroth*, angry; *chafing-dish*, a dish in which to heat water; *wist*, knew; *casement*, window; *dree*, endure; *boon*, a favour.

[160] There is uncertainty about whether or not this is a ballad in the true sense, although in the writing it is influenced by other ballads of the day. It is accepted by some as the earliest, but there is no known song version, and it is thought to be the work of a 'clerk' rather than of the 'folk'. There are many *Judas* legends, but this is the only one in which his sister appears. The original

text is to be found in a thirteenth-century manuscript in Trinity College, Cambridge. The version here is modernised.

Maundy Thursday, the Thursday before Easter when the ceremony of the washing of the feet of the poor is followed by gifts of clothing and money; *wist*—(if he) knew; *wreke*, angry; *i-take*, taken; *laved*, washed. The original text on which this 'ballad' is based is in the Gospel according to St.Matthew, chapter 26.

[161] Christopher Marlowe is famous for what Ben Jonson called 'Marlowe's mighty line'—meaning Marlowe's ability to write expressive, eloquent lines of poetry (especially in *Tamburlaine*). This excerpt from 'Doctor Faustus' catches the demented Doctor just before he is hauled into hell, having sold his soul to the devil for youth and absolute power. The Faustus legend is also the subject of a famous play by Goethe, the German poet, and of an opera by Gounod, the French composer.

O lente, lente, currite noctis equi!, O run slowly, slowly, horses of night; *Pythagoras' Metempsychosis*, Pythagoras, the Greek mathematician who lived in about the sixth century B.C., believed that after death, the soul passed into the body of another man or an animal; *Lucifer*, originally the name of the morning star, then given to Satan (the archangel cast out of heaven), hence the Devil.

[165] This ballad is based on the parable in the Gospel according to St. Luke, chapter 16, verses 19–25, in which another soul is dragged down to hell. People of the Middle Ages expressed their belief in hell in many ways, but none is more telling than that of the great sculptured doorways to the French cathedrals of Autun and Vézelay.

[173] The story of Samson is to be found in the Book of Judges—see especially chapter 16. *livery*, the uniform given by a person of rank to his servants; *cataphracts*, soldiers in full armour; *rifted*, split or tore apart; *assayed*, examined; *Philistian*, belonging to Philistia, the country of the Philistines, a war-like people who lived by the sea in south-west Palestine—now Israel; *vulgar*, the common people.

[178] *embalmer*, one who uses spices and preservatives to keep a dead body from decaying, as the Egyptians did; *benign*, kind, gentle,

well-meaning; *poppy*, from the seeds of which a drug called opium or heroin is obtained, and which when smoked or otherwise taken produces stupor, sleep, and insensibility; *wards*, locks.

[181] The original Thomas Rymer, Thomas of Erceldoune, lived in Scotland in the thirteenth century. He is believed to have written this story about a visit to fairyland. It is customary in such stories for the fairy folk to be described as wearing green clothes.

Huntlie bank, the bank of the river Leader, near Earlstoun; *ferlie*, wonder; *ilka tett*, every lock of hair; *siller*, silver; *louted*, bent, bowed down; *carp*, recite, often to the accompaniment of a harp; *weal ... woe*, well .. ill, good ... evil; *weird*, fate; *danton*, daunt, frighten, subdue with fear; *maun*, must; *braid*, broad; *lily leven*, white lawn; *brae*, hill; *aboon*, above; *mirk*, dark and gloomy; *stern*, star; *syne*, then; *pu'd*, pulled; *dought*, could; *tryst*, appointment to meet at a special time and place; *even cloth*, smooth cloth.

[186] *agate-stone*, a striped precious stone; *athwart*, across; *traces*, leather straps connecting a horse's collar to the waggon; *suit*, money paid for begging a favour of the sovereign at court; *tithe-pig*, one pig in ten paid to the church, or in payment of rent; *ambuscado*, ambush; *bake*, cake or matt; *elf-locks*, tangled hair.

[199] *after-damp*, the choke-damp left in a mine after an explosion.

[199] 'The Daemon Lover' is a traditional Scots ballad, although other versions are known widely in England, Ireland and America. It is the story of a man who returns from the dead to claim the girl he was once engaged to.

wad, would; *hae*, have; *yersel*, yourself; *kend*, knew; *baith*, both; *weel*, well; *taffetie*, silken cloth; *drumlie*, troubled; *ee*, eye; *cloven foot*, a foot divided length-wise like that of the cow, pig, etc. The god Pan is described by the ancient Greeks as having had such a foot: hence the myth that the devil too is cloven-hoofed.

[204] *gordian shape*, like that of the intricate knot tied by Gordius, King of Phrygia, and of which the gods declared that whoever was able to loosen it should be ruler of Asia. Alexander the Great cut it with his sword; *pard*, leopard; *penanced*, like one who intends to repent for wrong-doing; *Ariadne*, character in an ancient Greek myth whose husband placed among the stars the crown he gave her at their wedding; *tiar*, tiara, or ornamental head-band of jewels; *Proserpine*, or Persephone, the goddess who was carried off unwillingly to the underworld where she was forced to live for a third of the year, being allowed to return to earth for the remaining eight months, thus representing in myth the disappearance of flowers and other plants in winter and their re-appearance in spring.

[216] A poem from the Middle Ages. Where possible, the spelling of this version has been modernised.

hermitage, a lonely dwelling-place for men living away from the rest of the world; *hight*, called; *clerk*, one who could read the scriptures; *had much less of lore*, was not so well educated; *took them to rede*, took counsel or advice; *gan dwell*, went to live; *wistful*, mournful and longing for company; *felauhede*, companionship; *take heed*, pay him attention; *louted*, bowed low; *meek*, with gentle courtesy; *besought*, had asked for; *solace*, comfort; *semblance*, appearance; *high undurne*, the first prayer time (morning); *the nones*, the last prayer time (evening); *nere*, never; *mervaile*, marvel, wonder; *sooth to say*, truth to tell, truly; *a bear through kind*, it is the nature of the bear; *slo*, slay or kill; *plained him sore*, beat his breast, lamenting and weeping to show his pain and grief at the bear's death.

[230] 'The Odyssey' is the epic story of Odysseus, King of Ithaca in ancient Greece. After the fall of Troy he was forced by the gods to wander for ten years before he was able to return home. E. V. Rieu has made a prose translation of *The Odyssey* (Penguin Books, 1946) and of *The Iliad* (Penguin Books, 1950) which describes the Trojan War.

Parnassos, a mountain in central Greece, sacred to Apollo and the Muses, the nine daughters of Zeus who were the inspiration of poets and musicians; *Hélios*, the sun; *rune*, spell or magic charm; *stanched*, stopped; *repaired*, set off, made their way.

[233] *feverfew*, the plant pyrethrum; *red-nettle*, Common Pellitory-of-the-Wall, a bush member of the nettle family with reddish brittle stems, which grows in cracks in walls, once used as a favourite medicine.

[237] In 'The Poem of Ten Ones' the Chinese character for 'one' is used ten times: hence the title. *Ch'ing dynasty, 1644-1911.*

[241] *magnets*, to attract enemy arrows; *dynasties*, successions of rulers of the same family.

[246] The spelling has been modernised in this extract from Sir Thomas Malory's famous book, first printed by William Caxton in 1485. See also the poetic version, *Idylls of the King* by Alfred, Lord Tennyson: 'The Passing of Arthur', line 170 *et seq.*

    yede, went; *rede*, counsel, advice; *brast*, burst; *wit*, know; *hieth*, approaches; *lief*, well-loved; *wappe*, lap; *wanne*, ebb; *weened*, thought.

[249] In a footnote to this poem the translator, Arthur Waley, refers to the four lines beginning 'By the bridge there was a house', and writes: 'There is no trace of it left. This passage describes the havoc of war. The harvest has not been gathered: therefore corn-offerings cannot be made to the spirits of the dead.'

[250-254] These passages were written out of the personal experiences of people involved in the two major world wars. Wilfred Owen was killed in action in 1918. *In Parenthesis* is a book about the experience of one soldier in World War I during part of 1915 and 1916. The language in which the author writes of the shock and pain and bewilderment of the soldier in the front line is full of poetry. He conveys powerfully the innermost feelings and thoughts of men who had to live through experiences as horrifying as those depicted in medieval pictures of hell.

    By comparison with World War I, World War II involved not only fighting forces, but civilians also—especially in cities

which were bombed. Some of these, as in the poem by Yevtushenko, were very young.

[255] *Orcus*, hell.

[256] *twa corbies*, two crows; *makin' a-mane*, complaining, grumbling,.
gossiping together; *tane intae the tither*, one to the other; *gang*,
go; *ahint*, behind; *auld fail-dyke*, old wall made of turf; *wot*, know;
kens, knows; *hame*, home; *swate*, sweet; *hause-bane*, neckbone;
pike oot, pick out; *to theek*, to line with or thatch.

[257] *make*, mate; *pall*, fine cloth, often of purple, used to cover the
dead; *may*, maiden.

[258] 'A Lyke-Wake Dirge' (*lyke-wake*, body watching; *dirge*, a
funeral song) is a folk song which was collected in the seventeenth
century. It was sung around the body of the dead by the body-
watchers. In it no story is told, but instead its ritualistic rhythms
and repetitions evoke visions of both the saved (those who went
to Heaven) and the damned (those who went to hell). Throughout the song glimpses of dread tremble like shadows from the
flickering candles of the mourners. In his Serenade Benjamin
Britten has set this song to new music of such perfection that once
having heard it, it is difficult for the listener to separate his music
from the words. Even so, if it is chanted in the proper mournful
voice it will, on its own, produce a very spooky feeling in
performers and listeners alike.

 ae, one; *fleet*, a place where water flows, a creek (hence Fleet
Street in London); *whinny-muir*, heath or moor covered with
gorse bushes (*whinnes*) and other prickly shrubs; *hos'n* and *shoon*,
stockings and shoes; *nane*, none; *bane*, bone; *Brig*, bridge; *Purgatory*, a place (or condition) in which souls of the dead, on de-
parting this life, are cleansed by suffering before they are ready
to be received into heaven.

[268] This passage has been arranged from material in *Readings in
English History from Original Sources, Book III* (*1486–1688*) ed.
Morgan and Balley (Blackie) 1908. Further background material
can be found in *The Gunpowder Plot* by Hugh Ross Williamson
(Faber, 1951).

[268] *grounded*, firmly established; *Romanists*, members of the Catholic faith; *persecution of the Catholics*, during the seventeenth century Catholics were forbidden by law to practise their religious beliefs and many suffered imprisonment and death; *promulgated till*, publicly announced for.

[281] *silly*, humble, poor.

[288] *makèles*, matchless, peerless (pronounced as three syllables mak, è, les); *ches*, chose; *moder*, mother.

Index of Poets' Names

(With titles of poems. Where a poem has no title,
the first line is given in italics.)

Index of First Lines

Index of Titles